Street Children of Mongolia
A Perspective

Street Children of Mongolia

A Perspective

Maqsooda S. Sarfi

SHIPRA

Rs. 600; US$ 30

ISBN: 978-81-7541-722-9

First Published in India in 2014

Street Children of Mongolia: A Perspective

Published by:
SHIPRA PUBLICATIONS
H.O.: LG 18-19, Pankaj Central Market, Patparganj,
I.P. Ext., Delhi-110092, Tel: 91-11-2223 5152, 2223 6152
Br.Off.: 4617/18, Ansari Road, Darya Ganj,
New Delhi-110002, Tel: 9650028065, 9810522367
E-mail: info@shiprapublications.com
www.shiprapublications.com

Foreword

The welfare of children is one of the primary and basic duties of a state in its quest in building prosperous and affluent structures for the inhabitants of that state. The different organs of the UN, recognizing the 'child' as the most valuable entity, have not been only sensitizing the states about their responsibilities towards the rights of children, but have also launched numerous welfare programs for them.

The phenomenon of 'street children' in which children, who have not attained the adulthood, find streets as their home which equally provide a source of living for them and their families poses a new challenge. This phenomenon is a new menace for many in under-developed and developing country. In this behalf, Dr. Maqsooda's study relating to street children in Mongolia is a valuable contribution in comprehending the problem and devising solutions to deal with it.

The study provides a fascinating and scholarly backdrop of the socio-cultural and historical developments of Mongolia. The different historical phases through which Mongolia has passed provide deep insights to comprehend the present day menace of street children in that society. The author underlines the impact of disintegration of Soviet Union which led to the stunning socio-economic changes in the former USSR and its East European satellite States. The author rightly maintains that in the earlier system the state was solely responsible for the health care, education and employment of children. However, with the emergence of a new system, this cover of protection and care does not exist any more. This formulation, backed by empirical evidence on the part of the author, provides sociological insights of the new system which has emerged in Mongolia post-Soviet disintegration.

The author, evolving an insightful sociological framework, estimates the various political and sociological developments which took place in the Mongol society over the centuries. This approach has enhanced the credibility of the study. It is equally interesting to note the various stages, viz; nomadic, tribal, feudal, socialist and now the neo-capitalistic, through which the Mongol society has undergone over the long periods of its checkered history. This appraisal enables the reader to comprehend the impact of different social systems on its people.

The author has discussed in detail the changing social structures of Mongol society from time to time. This ongoing phase in the Mongol society has resulted in limited resources and shrinking subsidies.

The initiatives which have been taken by the International organizations and the Mongolian government itself in addressing the problem and rehabilitating the street children in Mongolia has been discussed and critically evaluated in detail. The policy recommendations proposed by the author should prod the policy makers in Mongolia towards some pragmatic action in addressing the problem.

I congratulate to Dr. Maqsooda for her contribution on the important subject for its historical, sociological and empirical approach.

Professor Riyaz Punjabi
Formerly, Vice Chancellor,
University of Kashmir,
Srinagar, Kashmir.
President (Hony.)
International Centre for Peace Studies,
New Delhi.

Preface

Though standing at great physical distance from each other with difficult overland connectivity, India and Mongolia both can rightfully boast of cultural and spiritual links traceable to distant antiquity. The Hun invasion of India in 3rd century BC saw settlement of some people of Mongoloid origin in parts of North and Northern India and the traces of Buddhism became manifestly visible in Mongolian cultural universe. The faith and philosophy of the Buddha perpetuated in Mongolia over the millennia, and braving many vicissitudes remains in place down to the present day. This interaction was highly beneficial in preserving ancient Indian learning in various branches in the shape of enormous translations in Mongolian called *Kanjur* (Buddhist Scripture) and *Tanjur* (Exegetical Works). Indian mission in Ulaanbaatar has done a commendable job of digitalizing these texts and preserving the fund for posterity. The impact of Sanskrit language on Mongolian dialects remains a vivid and successful story of cultural interaction between the people in ancient Asia. After her independence, India was the first country to formally recognize Mongolia as a sovereign state and formal diplomatic relations between the two countries were established in 1954. Thereafter a new and unprecedented chapter of bilateral relationship and cooperation between the two countries developed satisfactorily interspersed by exchange visits of high dignitaries from each country. Today India has extended the field of cooperation and assistance from training, scholarships, information technology, agriculture, e-governance to solar electrification, defence, trade and commerce.

Kashmir, too, had her share of relationship with Mongolia. Ancient Kashmir kingdom had trade relations with the Central Asian regions to the north and east from very early times and in fact Kashmir was connected by arteries across the eastern Karakorum (present day Ladakh and Shahidullah Pass) and Swat and Chitral (across the western Pamirs and Hindu Kush) linking it up with the ancient Silk Road. These routes also served the purpose of transmitting Buddhist teachings and ancient Kashmiri cultural traits and artifacts with strong Buddhist leanings. As a transit point and a centre for Buddhist learnings, Kashmir rendered remarkable service in disseminating the message of Buddha to Central Asia, Tibet and Mongolia. Among famous Kashmiri Buddhist scholars are celebrated Nagarjuna, Vasubandhu and Dignaga, whose texts also find place in the Mongolian translations of *Kanjur* and *Tanjur*. Hieun Tsang, the great Chinese traveler and Buddhist monk of the 7th century stayed for a long time in Kashmir. In later 13th and early 14th century, the vast empire of Chingiz Khaan was distributed among his successors and during the reign of Mōngke Khaan, some regional commanders around the Karakorum made some occasional forays into Kashmir mainland but did not establish a kingdom. During the reign of Ogdai Khaan, a descendent of Chingiz, Namu a Kashmiri Buddhist monk and his brother came to the imperial court. Ogdai's successor Mōngke appointed Namu Guo-shi or the state preceptor to look after religious affairs. Prof. Bira tells us that Namu received a jade seal as a symbol of authority from the Khaan and his assignment put him in charge of ten thousand Kashmiri families. The Centre of Central Asian Studies, University of Kashmir has given me this assignment to investigate the problem of street children of Mongolia, which is quite a new phenomenon in post 1991 Mongolian society. The institute caters significantly to the region that is contiguous to Kashmir in physical or cultural terms. In case of Mongolia, it falls within the ambit of Central Asia on the one hand and on the other we are also aware of a long history of relationship between India and Mongolia. We shall give a bird's eye view of the spectrum of relationship to justify our labour of conducting research into a phenomenon in a neighbouring country.

A decade is not even a twinkle in the context of historical process, but a single moment at times lets the society in motion and leaves indelible imprints on the future course of the history of the nations. Since 1990 Mongolia has changed and has made considerable progress. Thinking and values of Mongolian people have changed. Democracy and market economy has brought with it new opportunities as well as new problems alien to erstwhile socialist societies of USSR, Eastern Europe, Central Asia and the like. With the assistance of international community it came out of many grave problems in a short period of time and is on the path of democracy. Government shows considerable interest in reducing the poverty of its people. It has taken the initiatives in the projects, aiming to make weaker sections stand by their own and actively participate in the national building project of Mongolia. Currently, joint studies with the Non-government organizations for the assessment and dynamics of social problems, arising out of the re-structuring of Mongolian economic, political and social structure. Specific studies are conducted on the abuse and violence against children and their personality development. Re-structuring and associated forces have engulfed Mongol society. Besides tremendous activity on politico-economic front, cultural domain is no less transforming. Amongst various socio-economic problems emerging out of new system, the problem of street children is new social phenomenon with far reaching ramifications for human resource development and has serious concerns for Mongol national pride and identity. Agencies like National Child Protection, Social Welfare, UNICEF, UNDP, Save the Children Fund, Christian Noble Foundation, Police Department and Government plans hopefully to have no such children on the streets by 2012. They have been true to their commitment as we cannot see such children anymore on the streets. Cridet goes to the mining sector which brought tremendous investments from outside through which GDP has increased. According to the Tokyo television broadcaster Mr. Ohama Hiretaro, Mongolia was placed among the best three highest GDP countries in the world in his program called "Sekai o mite, Ashita o yomu" keizai "yosoku" (To predict future economy, through watching today's world) on August 26th 2013.

Although various research groups and individual researchers are contributing to the analysis of the new phenomenon, I am highly thankful to the Centre of Central Asian Studies, University of Kashmir which reposed confidence in my efforts and assigns a short time project with the main objective to sketch out the various dimensions of the problems. The Centre caters significantly to the region that has proximity to Kashmir in terms of geography and culture.

My sincere gratitude and thanks go to the Vice-Chancellor, University of Kashmir, Prof. (Dr.) Riyaz Panjabi whose encouragement made my return to the field of studies possible. I am indebted to Prof. Mushtaq A. Kaw, Director, Area Studies Centre, Center of Central Asian Studies, who has been instrumental in bringing me back to the center and giving me this assignment. I would like to thank Dr. G. M. Mir, Director, Center of Central Asian Studies, Dr. G. R. Jan, and Dr. Ajiaz A. Bandey for their support and encouragement. Thanks go to Mongolian former Ambassador Mr. Voroshilov Enkbold, First Secretary Ms. Dorlig Gerelmaa, Ambassador Mr. Sanjaasuren Bayaraa, Embassy of Mongolia in New Delhi for their arrangements to make my stay fruitful in Mongolia. I am grateful to Mr. Mustaq Halwai, Research Associate for his research inputs and arrangement of facts, besides going through the monograph. It is because of his humble efforts that the monograph is what it is. I would also like to thank Mr. Nazir Ahmad Doshab and Mr. Aftab Ahmad Hakim for helping me for many print outs and presentation of the monograph.

I am thankful to all the government officials and non-government organizations in Mongolia who made it possible for me to complete this work by their co-operation and understanding. My thanks goes to National Council for Children, implementing agency of the government of Mongolia, National Authority for Children, also Children Foundation Executive Director and Chairperson Mr. Togtokhnyam Mijiddorj, Ms. Darikhand Bayar, Mongolian Social Welfare (MSW) Child Protection Officer, UNICEF Office for Mongolia, Ms. Sasarma Psychologist Center Against Children's Violence, Save Children Fund Mongolia Director, Mr. Mitsuaki Toyada, Ms. Bolormaa Gulgou Child Protection Programme Officer, Ms. Munkhzul Khoovoi of Save Children Center and Mr. Purevhoshuuch, Children Identification Center, Prof. Shagdariin Bira, Secretary General of International Division Academy of Science, Dr. O. Nyamdawaa, Protocol Advisor of Ministry of Foreign Affairs, Dr. Sanjaasuren Oyun Minister of Nature, Environment and Green development, World Vision-Adiya Byambatseren and Mr. Mukul Dixit National Coordinator, Baigalmaa Sunren Head of the Coordination Department Municipality Authority for Children, Ulaanbaatar city. My excellent translator and interpreter Onon Bayasgalan and Mr. Amarsan.

I also owe my thank to close friends Ch. Burenbayar, Senior manager communication and media, Oyu-Tolgoi, LLC, Ulaanbaatar, UNICEF, Saranchmiig and Purevbaatar Luvsandavga Vice-Chairman Railway Authority who made my stay very comfortable and looked after all my needs. Mr. Sambudorj and his wife who accompanied me all the places deserve my thanks. I thank Dr. S. Talal for his humourous puns to keep my spirits high. My sister-in-law, Farida Sarfi deserve my special thanks. I am thankful to Shipra Publications especially Mr. D. Kumar for accepting this book for publication.

Last of all my thanks to my biggest strength – my children Rubina and Himayu who always stand by me and give me the immense pleasure of discussing issues with them.

Contents

1 Conceptualization of the Problem

The children are the hope and future of a nation, the most prized possession of a country, yet they happen to be the most vulnerable segment of the society. The children from the weaker sections of the society are particularly a miserable lot. They are deprived of the basic human rights, abused, discriminated against, forced to work, maltreated and mostly ignored, when their age demands care and attention. These children have been labeled as "street children"; a category of deprived who have neither shelter nor food. UNICEF defines street families as "those living and working on streets and a street child or youth is any girl or boy (under 18) who has not reached adulthood, for whom the street has become her or his abode and a source of livelihood, and who is inadequately protected, supervised or directed by responsible adults".[1] Street children include two categories referred to by UNICEF as "on the street" and "of the street". However 'street children' is specifically an urban phenomenon. Street children are totally on their own, living with other street children or homeless adult street people. These children probably lack parental, emotional and psychological support normally found in a secure home. Children on the street earn their living or beg for money on the street and return home at night".[2]

In some countries, including India, the problem of street children has a long history due to its social setup and demographic factors contributing to it. The street working children generate income for low income families. The faith becomes a factor that increasing population means more hands to work and more income. Street living children are those who work, sell or beg in the markets, are homeless and have no contact with the family. There are two categories of street children; one is street living and the other is street working. The later spent most of their time on the streets, fend for themselves but return home on regular basis but the former do not return home at all. The problem of street children is new in comparatively lesser developed countries of Eastern Europe, Central Asian States and in Mongolia, where this problem was non-existent during the socialist era as economy was regulated and there was well established social security net taking care of social welfare. Post-independence economic instability and transition to market economy rolled back this social security net and the problem of street children surged forth like a menace.

Withdrawal of Soviet Union subsidies, disruption of traditional COMECON (Council for the Mutual Economic Assistance) trade and reduced resources left the Mongolian government in lurch. To reduce the burden, Mongolian government took measures like, privatizing state owned assets, reducing or eliminating state subsidies causing unemployment, increasing stress level among bread earners which ultimately led to destabilization of established family patterns and adversely affected parental behavior, leading to the excessive alcoholism. With the financial insecurity the child abuse and abandonment increased among the families. Post-communist Mongolian cities particularly Ulaanbaatar witnessed a flood of street children, deprived of parental care and home. Soviet social engineering and its execution for a long period contributed negatively to the social problem, which in zeal to increase the population of the sparsely populated Mongolia, destroyed traditional family institution and reformulated value system to give social sanction to the birth of children out of wedlock. It hardly amounted to a social problem because state used to take care of this segment of society. When the system collapsed, the families as institution and parent as sources of legitimacy were unable to share the responsibilities. Besides, state for economic crunch and lack of institutional apparatus proved a failure to cope up with the new phenomenon.

UNICEF report indicates that about 45 per cent of the children in Mongolia choose street life by their own choice indicating the gravity of the breakdown of the families. The whole social structure got disrupted and it affected every field of life like, health, education, social service and infrastructure.

Mongolian government in collaboration with NGOs[3] and philanthropic societies has come forward to render help in solving this problem. National Center for Children, Save the Children Fund, UNICEF, World Vision, Christian Noble and many others have focused to reduce the poverty level and facilitate this deprived lot to have access to the basic social services. The National Programme of Action for the Development of Children in the 1990's took several measures for the improvement of these children. United Nations MDG (Millennium Development Goals) of 2002 and 2007 were set to give protection and rehabilitation to the children in difficult conditions.

Nonetheless, the continuous effort by the Mongolian government and NGOs are demonstrating strong commitment to solve this problem and with their efforts the number of street children has gone down. Picture does not look so gloomy now and continuous state action is encouraging and showing positive results.

PURPOSE/OBJECTIVE

The present book dwells mainly to the extent and nature of the new social phenomenon of street children of Mongolia. It simultaneously pinpoints main factors for its emergence and remedial measures of rehabilitation. Disintegration of Soviet Union led to the phenomenal socio-economic changes not only in the erstwhile USSR, but its aftershocks rippled across whole East European satellite states. The collapse released pent up forces in economic, social and political spheres as a result of liberalization from nearly seven decade old bastion of communist ideology and central command economic system. Dismantling of the iron curtain gave breathing space to long suppressed democratic aspirations on one hand but most of the constituent elements of great empire were besieged by an identity crisis. As no social movement or political struggle presaged independence, the freedom was more deserved than desired. Notwithstanding area study expert observations, the Soviet system was considered as welfare colonialism, quite different from European colonialism, particularly to the socially underdeveloped societies of Mongolia and Central Asia. In the seemingly classless society, elders and children were the most prestigious of classes. The system ensured care for children, their education, health care, employment and post-retirement benefits.

The whole Mongol social milieu underwent a transitional phase, which is always painful. New institutions started coming up. The older ones were either discarded or restructured to cope with new social realities. The problem suddenly emerged with all its dimensions, invoking scholarly interest to investigate this particular dimension of transition and its manifestations.

The purpose of this monograph is to present a snap shot of this appalling problem which demands remedial measures based on scientific analysis. The research problem for the present book is thus formulated and stated as the *Street Children of Mongolia: A Case Study of Ulaanbaatar.*

The present investigator is a frequent visitor to Mongolia, who observed the Mongolian society both before and after Soviet disintegration. The plight of the street children of varied ages and social backgrounds was appalling and their numbers were increasing during first five years of independence. Government and non-government agencies presented contradictory and confusing figures as regards their actual numbers. It varied from 1,000 to 10,000 in different reports.

The investigator's interaction with government and non-government agencies, UNICEF, Save the Children Fund, World

Vision, Christina Noble Children Fund, which were engaged in providing succor to this miserable lot, provided first hand background material to build a contextual framework and tentative hypothesis for the present monograph. It also proved fruitful to sketch out the objectives of the study, which are sated as under:

- To have an in-depth study of street children in their typical social set up;
- To assess the role of the government and non-government agencies with regard to the rehabilitation and education of street children;
- To suggest measures for the welfare of street children.

The purpose of this study is to take up just one aspect of the transformation of society in Mongolia. We are examining the impact of this transformation on the social structure, focusing on the children especially street children who are the product of this change. Mongol society has its own norms imbedded in their history. Post communism Mongol society was unable to cater for these children, owing to its shallow economy and broken family pattern. How then has the Mongol state dealt with the problem? This is precisely the question that we have tried to answer in this monograph. Research methods and generalizations can be replicated to the study of liberated societies in post-communist period only on a limited scale otherwise generalizations if any, pertain specifically to Ulaanbaatar. While dealing with the condition and status of street children of Mongolia, it seems essential to give some passing references to the geography and people in order to give a comprehensive understanding of the subject under investigation. Therefore, a brief geographical and historical frame is introduced to give glimpses of the Mongol social structure and value system, which in the first instance was instrumental in increasing the population of the region and legitimizing the children born out of traditional wedlock. The historical frame, therefore, is not only brief but was mercilessly passed through a sort of Kangroclosure, often disregarding normal historical procedures. Specifically the early historical portion was subjected to this procedure. Centuries seem to be squeezed in small paragraphs while maintaining the chronology of historical events. The new socio-economic compulsions associated with transition, capitalism and market economy forced this innocent lot to the streets. Mongolia being an ancient country with considerably significant role in world history has remained less known for various reasons including the fact that it is a landlocked sandwiched between two major powers namely Russia and China. Besides, its distant location, lingual difference and age old traditions of mixed economy gave it a distinctive remoteness.

While tracing the history of Mongolia during the Soviet period and focusing on the social structure, economy and culture, profound changes are quite manifest. It seems a march of nomadic society from its indigenous traditions to modernity under communist political establishment.

The primary issue that had to be taken into account was the deep social trauma after the fallout of Soviet system. In a bid to increase the population of the sparsely populated country, the family system had broken under the specific rules that governed the Mongol society during communist rule, which in a bid to increase working force, not only legitimized illegal marriages and sanctified children born out of wedlock, but mother hood of more children carried social appreciation and economic advantages. In the new system the helpless women overburdened with extra responsibilities and denied social security have abandoned their kids because of economic constraints. These children already out of home and their numbers now enormously grown posed the grave problem with which Mongolian government and society were faced at the post communist stage.

While working on this monograph, assigned by the Center of Central Asian Studies, I was able to make two short visits for field study in Ulaanbaatar to have interviews and onsite observations. I personally visited almost all the sites in Ulaanbaatar. I attended lecture series arranged by American Center in Mongolia through the instrumentality of *Mr. Glenn Mullin*, scholar of the Buddhist studies. Mongolian scholars and students in many ways helped me to analyze the developments, when something was beyond my access.

Besides noticing the new issues, I was fascinated by the new culture, music of the newly emerged cultural groups, newly emerged pubs, Indian, Japanese, Korean and Italian restaurants that are booming in Ulaanbaatar. Meeting with NGOs, interviewing different people including interacting with my former teachers, my friends (who have changed their professions), parliament members, protocol advisers and others was of great help and their inputs have added value to my investigations.

Since I have been a frequent visitor of Mongolia since my student days therefore language was not a barrier. Whenever I needed explanation my excellent interpreter *Onon Bayasgalans* (Personal Secretary to Ms. *Sanjaasurn Oyun* Parliament member to *Great Khooral* in 2009-2011) generously helped me. Her fluency in English enabled me throughout the interviews not to make mistakes as for as possible in the translations.

Ulaanbaatar was selected as the universe of study for being densely populated area of otherwise sparsely populated country. Secondly after the disintegration of old order a high rise of urbanization was witnessed and recorded which pulled large chunks of rural population to cities, particularly to Ulaanbaatar, which now has almost one half of the total population of the country. The population of the city is multi-ethnic and mixed one. Although there are no social categories in Mongol society, it is, however, markedly divided on economic basis. A multi-purpose cluster sampling method was applied to Ulaanbaatar city, which yielded two cluster's namely *Bayan Olgi* and *Bayan Zurikh*.

Besides observations and interaction with the street children and area experts, an interview schedule was devised to acquire relevant information, befitting the objectives of the study. The questions for the interview schedule were open ended. The selection, wording and order of questions and answers were carefully done. For the investigator the experts did standardization of the Mongolian language to convey and elicit accurate information. The interviews were done under longitudinal research design instead of cross sectional design i.e. the subject respondents were engaged more than once. As the segment of these children are provided day and night shelter by the government and non-government organization in cities, the investigator therefore interacted with the sample children in the streets as well in the rehabilitation centers in order to derive accurate results. The investigator's command on local language and sensitivity to the local culture helped in the formulation of friendly rapport, resulting in rich response rate. The field study was launched in the month of October 2009 and its first compilation completed in the month of March in 2010 which after more inputs is now published in the form the present book.

In short, background knowledge, field study, interaction with relevant people, observations and snowball interaction during sit in situations comprised the instruments of methodology and employed for acquiring data for this monograph. Although investigator has humbly tried to make the monograph more analytical where variables of transition, economy, family breakup and cultural norms correlate with the problem under investigation, however, given the scope and nature of the monograph, it is more descriptive than analytical. I have confidence that the information I have been able to present is to a great extent factual and realistic with the purpose that any solution based on this study will go a long way in alleviating the suffering of street children of Mongolia and will be a way forward for similar looking social problems being faced in the developing and under developed parts of the globe.

NOTES

1. www//http//mexico-child-link.org/street children definition.
2. UNDP (n.d) Mongolia(2007) National Report.
3. In 1993 Japanese Women's Association of the Universities, Kanazawa send sewing machines, notebooks and second hand clothes to the President of Central Council of Mongolian Women's Federation who distributed them among 70 poor families.

Mongolian Dominant Features 2

BRIEF GEOGRAPHICAL FRAME

The Mongols with their Steppe traditions have fascinated the world ever since the beginning of civilization. Mongolia lies in the northern part of Central Asia, sandwiched between the two big powers Russian Federation on its north and Peoples Republic of China on its east, west and south. Geopolitically and geographically it belongs to both North East Asia and Central Asia. As in the past so in the present Mongolian geographical location has made it significant not only to China and Russia but also to the United States, Japan and South Korea that have emerged her economic neighbours while India since ages has been its spiritual neighbour.[1] Mongolia covers a total of 1.5 million square km, half of the size of India with a very small population of 2.7 million. Much of Mongolia consists of Steppes. Steppes with forest cover in the central part are well developed and the largest agricultural activity is concentrated in this area. It has Gobi Desert to its south and cold mountainous regions to its north and west. The country has an extreme continental climate, with long winters and short hot summers. The rigour of the cold climate is to some extent compensated by 260 sunny days with clear cloudless sky. That is why the country is called "*Khokh Tengeriin Oron*" land of

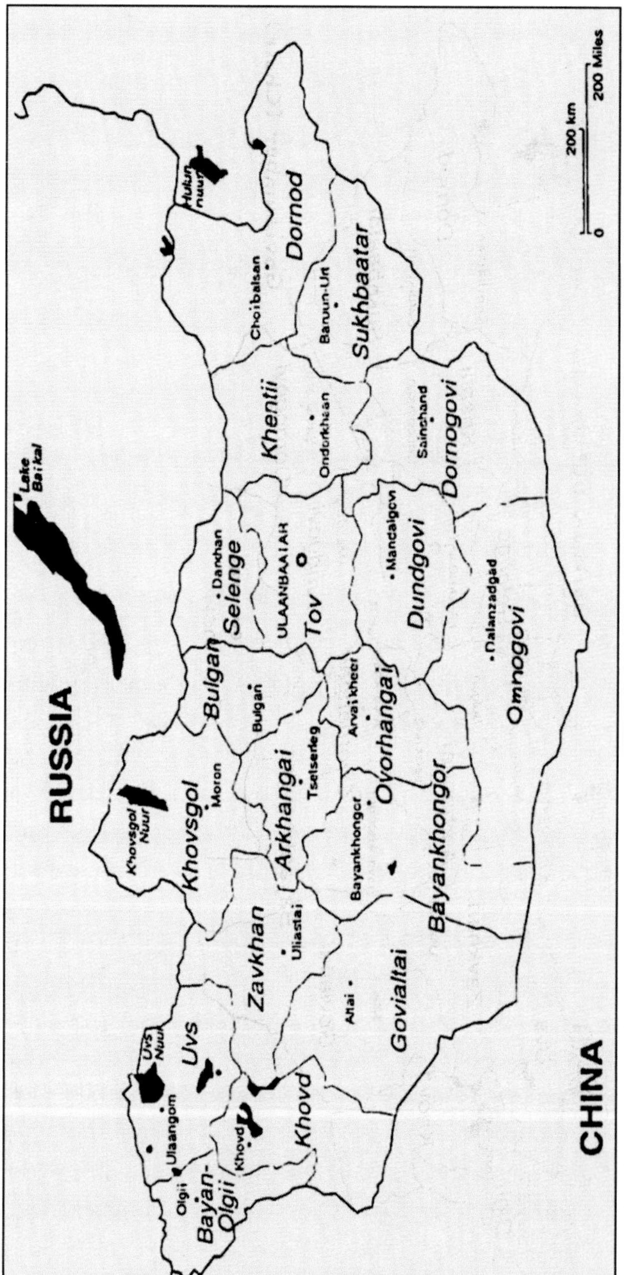

Source: Based on the map from Bruun, O. and O. Odgaard, Mongolia in Transition, Nordic Institute of Asian Studies: Curzon Press, 1996.

Fig. 2.1: Administrative units in the socialist period

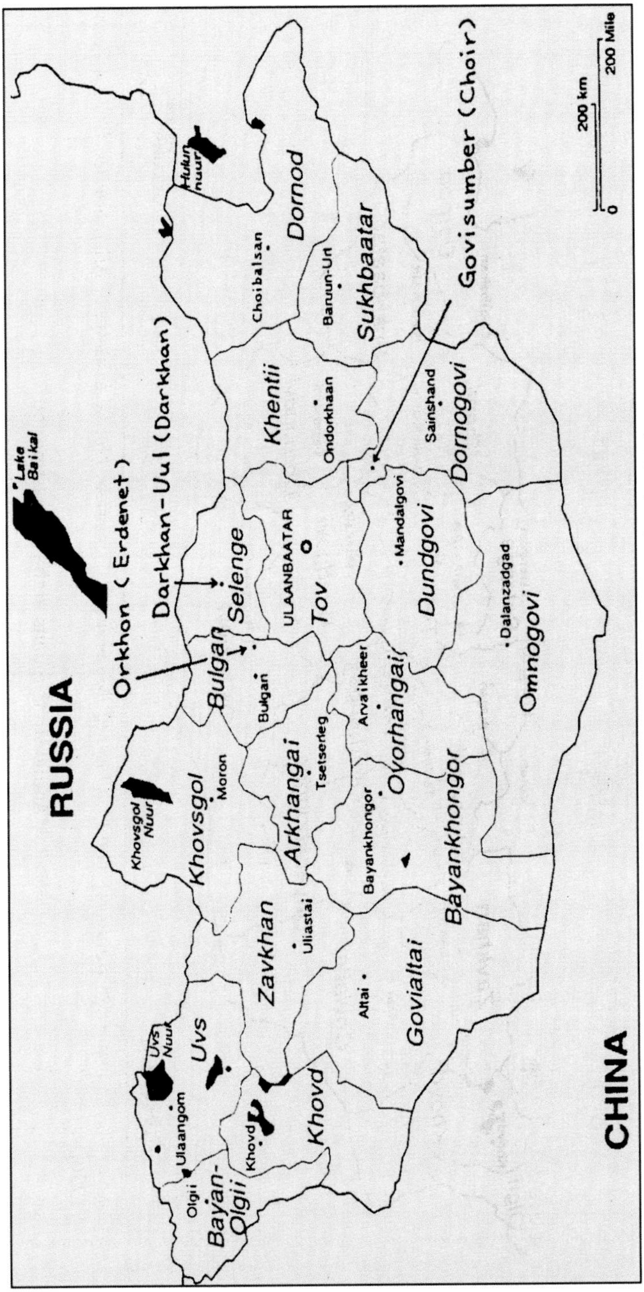

Fig. 2.2: Administrative units today (1994-)

blue sky. It is extremely cold in the winter which spans from November to March.[2] In northern part of the country, the average temperature in January is –34°C. The large part of the country lies at an altitude of 1000 to 2000 meters above the sea level. The shortest distance to the sea is 700km eastward through China to Yellow Sea.

In the socialist period, Mongolian People's Republic was divided into 18 *Aimages,*[3] with three large cities, the Capital Ulaanbaatar, Darkhan and Erdenet. After the independence slight changes started creeping in. In 1996 three cities Darkhan, Erdenet, and Choibalsan were turned into three new *Aimages* renamed as Darkhan-Uul, Orkhon and Govisumber respectively raising the number to 21*Aimages*. *Aimags* are divided into 328 *Soums* (districts) *Khoroo* (sub-districts) or *Baghs* (rural sub-districts), (Fig. 2.2). The Prime Minister appoints the chairman of the *Aimage*.

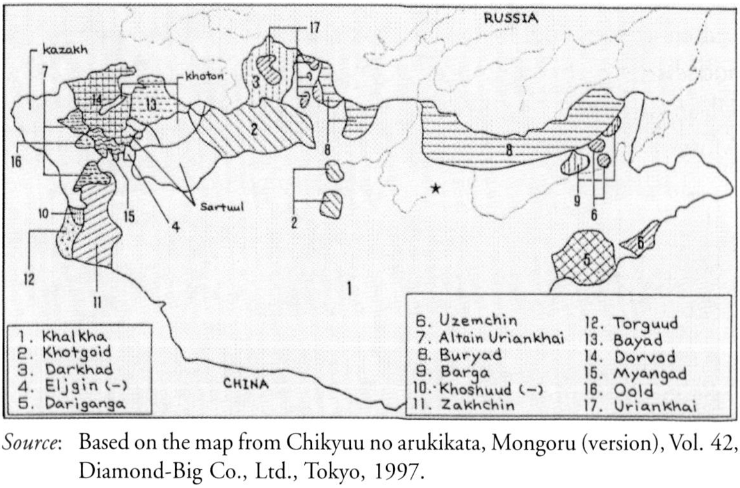

Source: Based on the map from Chikyuu no arukikata, Mongoru (version), Vol. 42, Diamond-Big Co., Ltd., Tokyo, 1997.

Fig. 2.3: Distribution of the Mongols

The periodic and non-periodic nomadic migrations, wars and mutual feuds across the region have resulted in vast intermixing of people. Consequently many tribal names occur in Central Asia as well as in Mongolia. Over 90 per cent of the population is made up of subdivisions of the Mongolian people, out of which *Khalkha* Mongols constitute about 86 per cent. The other ethnic groups are Kazakhs in the west and *Buryats* in the north. Besides, there is sizeable portion of *Dorvod, Oold, Bayad, Zakhin, Uriankhai, Barga* and *Kalmyk* ethnic stocks.

Surprisingly the Mongol diaspora living outside Mongolia is larger than the population inside Mongolia. In China population of Inner Mongolian Autonomous Region is about 3.5 million and in Russia it is about one million mostly living in *Buryat* and *Kalmyk* region. Presently children and youth under 35 make up 70 per cent of the population and the average age is 21 years. Out of 2.7 million populations about half live in cities and towns while the remaining 47 per cent still live in rural areas characterized by typical nomadic lifestyle. More than half of the urban population live in Ulaanbaatar alone.[4] Ulaanbaatar population has rapidly increasing as a result of urbanization and rush of population from rural areas and provincial centers to the capital city. The two years of *zudd* (snow storm) has added to the atrocities of rural people forcing them to migrate to Ulaanbaatar.[5] In 2009, 30000 livestock was lost due to the *zuud.* Most of the migrants live in *gers.*[6]

Fig. 2.4: Rural Nomadic Ger (Photo by Author)

Mongols have great love for their animals as their life style depends on these animals. Although Soviet planned economy brought urbanization yet Mongols retain their nomadic herding style, moving from one place to other in search of green pastures for their animals. The five kinds of domestic animals, horse, cow, camel, sheep and goat are very important in their daily life. These five are called *tavan khoshuu mal.* The names for them vary with their age and sex. For example, horses are shown as Table 2.1.

General term		Aduu
Male	Breeding	*Azraga*
	Castrated	*Mori*
Female		*Guu*
One year old		*Unaga*
Two year old		*Daaga*
Three year old		*Shudelung*
Four year old		*Khyazaalang*
Five year old		*Soyoolong*

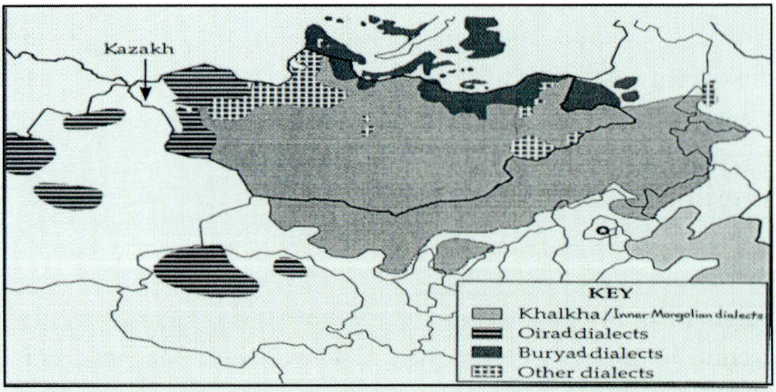

Source: Bruun, O. and O. odgaard, Mongolia in Transition, Nordic Institute of Asia Studies: Curzon Press, 1996.

Fig. 2.5: Distribution of the Mongolian language

From the linguistic point of view, Mongolian language is said to belong to the Altaic group of languages together with Turkic and Manchu-Tungusic. The language spoken by Mongols is *Khalkha,* which is the standardized official language of Mongolia. It has a rich nomadic vocabulary and is generally understood by all Mongols, used in everyday life, in administration, education, books and newspapers. Presently both the Cyrillic and old Mongolian scripts are used in schools. Besides *Kkalkh* dialect, Turkic speakers (Kazak, and Tuvans) make up of 5 per cent and small portion speaks Russian, Chinese and English.

BRIEF HISTORICAL FRAME

Mongols emerged as a dominant tribal confederation between eleventh and twelfth centuries though the history of Mongols is said to have originated from the formation of a social group in the 3rd century BC under the Huns, who played a significant role in the social and political history of Euro-Asian nomadic tribes. Mongolia has been the home of one of the three most important ethnic groups of the world, namely the Mongoloid, the Xian'pi and the Hun. In 4th century the Jujan, ethnically close to the Xian'pi, assumed the title of Khagan. The Jujan led a nomadic way of life, raising livestock, growing some crops and living in round felt tents. They maintained diplomatic relations with Central Asia, Chinese ruling dynasties and Korea. Jujan were replaced by the Turk, whose political history was extraordinarily stormy and due to the internal strife, they broke up at the end of the 6th century. They were replaced by the Uighur Khaganate, who invented their own Uighur script based on Sogdian. By the end of the 8th century their decline led their merger into the Kirgiz Khaganate, whose writ lasted only for short period and were eventually driven out by the Kitan. These ethnic Mongols during 10th-12th centuries stretched their territorial boundaries up to the North China and their rule is characteristic progress in the field of art, science, education and religion. But in 1125 this empire declined due to internal fueds.

In 12th century a feudal mode of production emerged among the tribal conglomerates and it was the period when first Mongol *Ulus* (tribe) was formed under the *Khabul Khagan*, who ruled the

Khamag Mongol *Ulus (Mongolian State).* This was the largest tribe who lived on the banks of the *Onon*, the *Kherlen* and the *Tuul.* The other tribes were the *Krides*, who inhabited the area between *Khangai*and *Khentii* mountain ranges. The *Naiman,* lived near *Khangai* and *Altai* mountain ranges, the Tatars were in the *Khulun Buir*, the *Merged* in upper reaches of the *Selenge* river and the small tribe of *Onguut* were under the suzerainty of *Ching* emperor of China.

During the 12th and 13th centuries, Mongol tribes continued their infighting. Domestic slavery promoted the interest of economically strong and rich families, who in turn played an important role in the process of forming a typical stratification among the nomads. Under these circumstances, in 1206, the feudal nobility on the banks of the Onon proclaimed Temujin as supreme ruler of the unified Mongol state and conferred on him the title of Chingiz Khaan. Mongol *Ulsu* (tribe) under the leadership of *Temujin* and his descendants managed to keep its roots anchored over such a vast area for about more than six centuries. Under Chingiz Khaan they gradually stepped in Europe and knocked at the doors of the mighty empires and subjugated them.

Apart from the great misfortune and destruction in men and material of conquered nations, it certainly did play a great role in socio-cultural development of the vast region. Mongol rule brought the East and the West closer not only in trade but also in the field of culture through which free flow of ideas passed among the nations, thus helped in forming the common cultural values. Through conquests a large part of the world was united into one single kingdom bound by appendages. Post conquest period has been highly acclaimed for overall security of the region, resulting in a conducive atmosphere for trade and commerce over Silk Route which accelerated civilizational march.

Keeping in view the significance of trade for the state, Khaan's missions went to every nook and corner long before the subjugation of territories. The big chunk of Khaan's missions was usually chosen from amongst the most popular lot of the society such as dancers, jugglers, performers who were most likely to have closer and better access to common man. Mongol disintegration started gradually for a number of reasons. Collapse of the Yuan dynasty divided Mongols into two major groups, eastern Mongols and *Oirad* Mongols in the west. In 1688, *Oirad* sought alliance with *Manchus,* who they thought were similar in religion, customs and language. This alliance is known as *Doloonnuur* convention of 1691. In 17th century *Manchus* established the Qing dynasty in China and brought under their sway various groups of Mongols except the *Buryat* and *Kalmyk* who were left to the Russian Empire. Under the Manchus both Inner and Outer Mongolia embraced Tibetans version of Buddhism and declared Mongolia as a Buddhist nation. Mongols were exploited in the name of religion but eventually this policy of Manchu's was largely responsible for the emergence of the independent movement of 1911, which won them independence under their religious leader, the eighth *Jebtsundamba Hutag (Bogd Gegeen*). He was crowned head of the church and state, with the title of "Elevated by All".

Till the revolution of 1921, Tibetan Buddhism chiefly characterized by Lamaism constituted an integral part of Mongolian culture and clergy managed to accumulate a large portion of the country's wealth. A theocratic state within the state with its own aristocracy and its laws, property and customs became a major feature of Mongolian society which to some extent succeeded in uniting all parts of Mongolia: *Khalkh*, Inner Mongolia, *Barga* and *Uriankhai* into one state. But Tsarist Russia was averse to the idea and recognized the autonomy of only Outer Mongolia in 1912. In 1913 a treaty was signed between Yuan Shikais and Tsarist government, by which Russia recognized the suzerainty of China over Mongolia and Mongolian territory as a part of China. In 1914 once again a meeting was arranged among Russia, China and Mongolia but the dream of unified Mongolia was not accomplished. It was during this period that present day geo-political division of Mongolia into Inner and Outer Mongolia was endorsed forever.

In 1921 Russian Red army helped Mongolia win its independence and in 1924 Outer Mongolia was declared Mongolian Peoples Republic, which lasted till 1990. Buddhism was so imbibed in Mongol psyche that even atheist party members had to respect the sentiments of the *Arats* and considered the monks as next to God. Therefore, *Bogd Gegeen* was made the nominal head of the state with limited powers. It was made clear that the church was not redeemable and would eventually be challenged and finally destroyed. Constitution gave full freedom of religion to all citizens of Mongolia but at the same time religious affairs were separated from the state.

In 1930 Japan sponsored a pan-Mongolian movement. Stalin regarded their presence in Manchuria a threat to the security of East Asia. In 1939 Mongolian-Soviet army defeated Japanese Mongolian troops. Inner Mongolia became autonomous regions of China and in 1947 China recognized Mongolian Peoples Revolutionary Party (MPRP) as the only representative organ of the State. At the eve of independence in 1950 Choibalsan succeeded in keeping Mongolia an independent state by a policy of friendly attitude towards Soviet Union until his death in 1952.Tesdenbal's tenure was marked by increasingly close relations with the USSR and institutionalization of a command economy in Mongolia.

From 60's onwards Mongolia focused mainly on the consolidation of socialist sector bypassing capitalism. The whole socio-economic setup was restructured on USSR pattern and the private property became its first causality. Foreign capital was ousted from the country's economy, foreign debt was annulled and a special state control was imposed on foreign trade and financial loans. Instead a cooperative and state trade was created. The foundation of national industry was laid and the first mechanized transport and communication centre was created. This played a decisive part in strengthening the country's productive force and its economic independence.

In 1961, Mongolia entered the Council for Mutual Economic Assistance (CMEA) which integrated Mongolian economy into the Soviet planning system, providing Mongolia with a large market for her exports, a secure supply of required imports and exceptionally favourable terms of trade. Its foreign policy also remained subservient to USSR and consequently the relations with China were strained.

The rivalry between China and Russia over Mongolia was a blessing in disguise. As both the countries wanted to get hold of Mongolia, therefore both tried to please Mongolia by providing two most important requisites of socio-economic development: capital and technical knowhow. Aids and loans led to the rapid development of infrastructure in Mongolia. China's strong desire of winning over Mongolia, forced Mongolia to seek more protection from Soviet Union. Consequently in 1970 Soviet troops were sent to Mongolia after the Sino-Soviet clashes. In 1980 trade relations between the two started improving and from 1985 to 1988 border trade and technological exchanges were rejuvenated. The system of trade between the two countries was based on border and barter. Mongolian and Chinese traders exchanged consumer goods of daily use through the Inner Mongolian border towns of *Erlian* and Chinese *Zamiinuud.*

Soviet Union took full advantage of the strategic location of Mongolia and used it as a buffer state against China and any possible threat of Japan. It also utilized its raw material for trade surplus. But at the same time it played significant role in the development of human resources, social progress and building of a totally new work culture in Mongolia. It was an uphill task for the new government to transform the nomadic society characterized by a traditional social, economic and political setup. Mongolia with a small literate population, a social order based on strong kinship institution across the vast steppe, with a limited communication and transport system, had to change. Most of the population lived semi nomadic way of life, continued with few other pursuits. There were no middle class or urban class of Mongols except the foreigners, especially Chinese and Russian merchants who were running the urban economy. The newly formed government had no option but to seek help either from Russia or China. Tsedanbal, who had Russian wife preferred to model its policies on Soviet pattern.

Throughout his presidency, Tsedenbal played the powerful China card whenever and wherever he needed the assistance from Soviet Union. Tesdenbal was removed from the office in 1984 and more liberal Batmonkh was elected as general secretary, who tried to implement the policy of economic restructuring as well as political openness but failed to do so during his five years rule from 1984-1989.

With the rise of Gorbachev as the Soviet leader, tension eased and in 1986, diplomatic relations were established between China and Russia. As a result withdrawal of Russian troops from Mongolia was made possible. In 1987, Mongolia and United State of America established diplomatic relation after a long break. The State visit of James Baker, US Secretary of State to Mongolia in 1989 further strengthened the relations; both in politics and economy. James Baker for the first time used the term third world neighbour which Mongolian government used for its future relations with the countries who supported Mongolia for experimentation in democracy and facilitated its transition to market economy[7].

Gorbachev's introduction of glasnost or "*il-tod*" and perestroika in Soviet Union and democratic changes in Eastern Europe helped to create a favourable open environment in Mongolia. The new generation of Mongolia who were educated and trained mostly in Soviet Union and Eastern Europe, soon demanded a change in political power as they too were influenced by the latest developments in these countries. First mass demonstrations of 1989 for the end of communist rule and formation of new democratic government paved the way for a change.

By late 1990 Soviet Union was busy with its internal problems and there came an obvious lull for Mongolia in its economic and political dependence on erstwhile Soviet Union. Mongolian new constitution declared that Mongolia will maintain friendly relations with the Russian Federation and the People's Republic of China who was fast growing as an Asian economic giant. Besides, it will develop friendly relations with developed countries of west and east. With this policy Mongolia rapidly enlarged its partnership of foreign trade with more than 66 countries instead of doing business with some 20 countries before the mid 1980's, mainly member countries of the CMEA led by Soviet Union.

Mongolia experienced a comparatively conducive political atmosphere as all the rival political parties and movements of reform showed great restraint in addressing the reform challenges, without putting national security and independence in jeopardy. The reform process had been both an event with far reaching consequence and remarkably peaceful in nature, compared to the political climate prevailing in neighbouring countries of Central Asia.

In 1990 Mongolia held its first free election in eighty years of modern history and has taken important steps towards the development of multi-party, pluralistic and democratic society. In 1992 Mongolia adopted her first democratic constitution, which outlined the country's major task to build a democratic, secular society, which would fully respect human rights and freedom. Through 1993 elections the first democratically elected president was installed, thus paving way for the establishment of new political structure. Under the allegation of corruption in high echelons of power, lawlessness and economic instability the president was forced to resign.[8] In 1996, 75 years uninterrupted rule by MPRP was over with the landslide victory of democratic coalition. The new coalition took upon the task of restructuring and genuine reforms. In this regard the international community of aid donors emerged as important factor in domestic policy making, extending for beyond the economic sphere, maintaining a considerable pressure on the government in the direction of continued democratization.

The name of the country was changed from Mongolian People's Republic to Mongolian *Ulus;* exhibiting a fundamental reversal and refutation of state managed historiography. The historical role of

Chingiz Khaan was re-evaluated. Before the democratic reforms great Khaan was described as a bloodthirsty and aggressive feudal lord, whose name was a taboo and people were afraid to even mention his name in public. The secret police in the "*dotood yaam*" (Ministry of Interior) were present everywhere to campaign against it. History text books considered him as a conqueror that brought misfortune and sufferings to other nations. Now he is re-casted as a historical figure, a hero and symbol of Mongol identity and unified Mongol nation. His portrait can be seen widely across the country – a great Khaan revisiting Mongolia.

Fig. 2.6: Statue of Chingiz Khaan Symbol of Mongol Identity (Photo by Author)

Fig. 2.7: From Selenge River to Chingiz Khaan (Photo by Author)

In common parlays Chingiz Khaan to Russians is a destroyer to Chinese originator of Yuan dynasty and to Mongols the founder of their independent statehood and a source of inspiration. The palace of *Chingiz Khaan* was built in Ulaanbaatar which developed as a great picnic spot for tourists. The name of the hotel was changed from *Selenge* River to *Chingiz* due to the rapid rise of Mongol nationalism and identity construction project.

SOCIO-ECONOMIC PROFILE

Mongolia had a nomadic tribal culture, with its literary language that enabled all the Mongol groups to communicate. The pastoral economy remained the same since its establishment as a tribal state with a slight difference in its regional character. Buddhism or Lamaism played a great role in bringing whole Mongol community together, characterized by some common features of culture which strengthened them in throwing the foreign Manchu's out of power.

Having come into contact with many civilized nations through conquests, Mongols could reap the benefits of commercial and agricultural endeavours. Gradually the Mongol way of life transformed which was regulated for the first time by "*Yasa*" prescribing definite norms for social and religious life in addition to the establishment of a political structure. With the advancement in the settled life, Mongols surpassed the civilized sedentary states in grandeur and cultural advancement.

The family structure of traditional Mongol society essentially took into consideration that it would be inconvenient for the entire joint family to stay in one *ger* (tent). This tendency undermined the value associated to joint family structure. However, kinship affiliations were called upon during distress for mutual help and cooperation strengthening extended pattern instead of joint pattern. As the eldest and the younger sons grew, got married and established their independent family units, they had to move out and take a new abode along with the share of herd. The youngest son retained the right to stay on and own ancestor *ger*. This system finds its roots in the ancient patriarchal system in which the father maintains his supremacy as long as he is alive and then passes it on to his youngest son. Traditionally youngest son inherits the *golomt* (hearth) while the elder son and the daughters go out to establish new family units. The hearth is physically located at the center of the *ger* hence the youngest son becomes the '*ezen*' (head) of the ancestral property[9]. This system was in vogue since Chingiz Khaan unified the hordes in one *ulus* (state). There was marked stratified society comprising of wealthy cattle breeders, warlords, pastoral nobility and *noyons*. They had different titles like, *baatar* (hero), *Sechen* (wise), *mergen* (sharp shooter) *bilge* (wise) and *bokh* (strong man). *Noyon* and *nokurs* was a new privileged class. They were exempted from taxes and had full share of the booty acquired from the vanquished people. They were also free from any kind of punishment. According to these laws the *arats* were obliged to take permission from their masters to join other nobles and the people captured from the conquered countries had to join the military services whenever required. There was a well-established slave institution – an important component of economy, pastoralist and military bureaucracy.

In Yuan dynasty, Buddhism played a great role in strengthening the feudal class. As the ruling dynasty gave special privileges to the Buddhist clergy so in return high ranking monks helped them in exploiting the common masses. Buddhist religious establishment was given land and was exempted from all taxes. Between 14th and 16th centuries the condition of the slaves remained unchanged. The cattle breeders dealt with livestock economy and could put pasture land into agricultural use only subject to the permission sought from their feudal lords. Decedents of greet Khaan formed a prestigious class known as *tsagaan yastan taijis*. This class was sub-divided into two: one the nearer decedents and the other supposed to provide military and monetary support to the Khaan. The *arats* were dependent on their *ezen* lords for building yurts, borrowing money etc. They had to consult *ezens* even in their private matters like marrying children.

They had to take permission to graze their cattle on the pastures as the *ezen* had fixed the places of grazing grounds for these *arats*. Among the *arat*s there were privileged and unprivileged classes. The most privileged class was that of the *darkhan* (craftsmen), who by their skill of work for nobles distinguished themselves from other common *arats*. This class was exempted from taxes and punishment in specific offences. The other class under the canopy of *sarats* included *Sain khun* (high-class wealthy people), *dund khun* (well to do), and *khar khun* (the lowest) and who served in the household of the feudal nobles.[10]

Manchu's divided these people into three classes as *albat arats, khamjilga arats* and *shavinars*. The *albat arats* were controlled by the rich feudal lords, had to pay taxes and provide military services for the upkeep of the *aimags* and *khushuus* banners. They had to offer gifts and bear expenses for the travel of the high ranking lamas and feudal lords from Lhasa to Peking. They were also obliged to look after the livestock of the lords and provide food and horses for postal services. *Khamjilga arats* were liable to annual taxes, the rate of which was fixed by law in the form of livestock and livestock products to the *taijis*. They had to work in their households and pay their debts. The Manchu government encouraged the high-ranking lamas to reduce *arat* population to bondage. These *arats* called *shavinars* had to look after the monasteries and monasteries' livestock; were obliged to provide fund, out of their personal belongings for construction of monasteries. The skilled personnel, artists, painters and craftsmen were used for religious art and building monasteries. Besides paying taxes to the monasteries' treasury, people had to pay some ritual offerings also to the holy mountains and *Bogd* Mountain. The personal serfs had to pay the taxes of their land owners. Monasteries possessed enormous wealth and had the right to rule over secular population within their monasteries' territory.[11] However, the socialist period gave a death blow to the traditional Mongol stratification and *ezen* institution. Until early 20th century Mongols had no concept of owning land and property. Their property always remained in livestock and their movements centred on their herds and herd products, climate and seasonal migrations in search of green pastures.

The family pattern revolved round pastoral economy and the family members remained close so that they could help each other in looking after the herds. Socialist period institution of *Khot-ail* (group of families) and *neg nutgiin Khun* (from the same town) were abolished after the collectivization. Livestock was nationalized and *negdels* were formed where different families worked together. All the family members became the card holders of the *negdels.*

Economic overhauling during socialist rule with rapid industrialization, gave inputs to the establishment of an urban society, dominating all spheres including economy, politics and civic affairs. Apparently the official ideology did not recognize any class except socialist working class, however, when keenly observed, the Mongol society from 1960 onwards with the rapid industrialization, witnessed a new privileged class called *ajilchiini,* who were closely related with Soviet industry ideology and life style. Mongol society was stratified in hierarchies according to their economic, social and political status. *Ajilchiini* turned to be a primous-inter-paras alongwith communist elite in the so-called classless society.

On the top of the hierarchy were the people who managed the country and were holding the reins of the power. They were known as *tsagaan*g (white collar) workers. They enjoyed all the privileges which otherwise were not meant for the rest of the population. The common people or the workers were known as *khokh* (blue) collar people. The ruling class was further classified as per the role of the individual. Trustworthy party members, working class, cooperative herdsmen and intelligentsia were accorded power and prestige accordingly to their status.

Membership in the party was essential condition for everyone who wished to pursue a professional career in any branch of economy or production. This apparatus was called *Ariin Khaalag* (rear door) and any person who had access to the rear door could get anything done. Card holder of the party enjoyed the benefits of the state, but they were also instrumental in extending the privileges to their friends, relatives or their acquaintances. Thus any link with the card holders was a key to success and it was over and above the party consideration. A complex nexus of patronage and loyalty was in full swing in Soviet Union, Eastern Europe, Central Asia and Mongolia.

The workers and members of the MPRP were trusted ones and were provided all the facilities such as good accommodation, highest position in the administration, good health care and their children were sent to the best universities in foreign lands. The people who were not the party members were always under the fear of secret police. The secret police kept an eye on the activities of these people and if found criticizing government policies, were sent to remote areas. Anything against government or party was taken as an offence punishable by law.

The managerial elite, technical specialists, engineers, doctors, professors and financial planning experts were significant strata in the hierarchy. The urban elite were fluent in Russian and were trained in Soviet universities. In 1970-1980's it was the order of the day to inquire whether a person knows Russian or not.[12] Students from segments of herdsman, industrial workers and intelligentsia were sent to Soviet Union to study the language. While studying in Soviet Union most of them married Soviet women which in due course of time turned into a status symbol, commanding respect. However, marrying a Chinese girl was still considered a taboo and discouraged by overt and covert means.

During the Manchu period lama population renounced their sexual and reproductive rights to their own women. Alongwith a sizeable portion of unmarried Mongolian women, these renounced ones had to find other partners. Single Chinese male segment coming to Mongolia for trade provided potential alternatives. This largely changed the contours of Mongol social life and family pattern. As a policy matter Manchu did not allow the married Chinese traders to take their wives to Mongolia to ensure their return. Manchu law prohibited Chinese merchants and traders taking their families to

Mongolia lest they stay on for good. Again, the same law put restrictions on taking Mongolian wives to China. Nevertheless, these laws did not stop men and women from finding a partner, even temporarily. A large number of lamas and Chinese traders are reported to have developed sexual relationships with Mongolian women. The children born out of this illegal relationship were denied legitimate parenthood and this phenomenon led to a serious social problem for Mongolia in the long run. Single mothers brought up the children born outside wedlock with foreigners as these were not supposed to go with their fathers. Foreigners were subjected to many restrictions of travel and movement. These usually stayed in urban centres but such restrictions did not apply to the monks who were free to travel in Mongolian rural areas. Between 1930 and 31 military service was made compulsory for the high lamas and they had to pay stipend for the lamas who remained in the monasteries to serve them.

For the economic progress under Socialist period all the *shaivenar* (*Buddhist disciples*) were organized into local regional and political districts with their own elected representatives. Land and livestock was nationalized; companies were established to collect the cattle and other kind of property from the monasteries. *Arats* were allowed to use pastures freely; the confiscated livestock from monasteries was given to the *serfs* and *shivnars* who used to tender the herds and pastures of the nobles and monasteries. Lamas were punished and sent to prison if they violated the law on religion. Common people were forbidden to pay any kind of money for the building of new monasteries and lamas were not allowed to travel to the country side without prior permission. A considerable advance was made from rural animal breeding economy to an agro-industrial economy. The government succeeded in establishing sedentary life in the big cities but in rural areas it was hard to do so as nomads were always on the move for greener pastures.

A whole generation, born in fifties was made to sever links with the nomadic life style, as they were brought up in the cities and educated in USSR and Eastern Europe. Ironically this class gave lip service to official doctrine of socialism and state polices. It was this generation which became instrumental in seeking change in the political setup of Mongolian society.

A new working class and working intelligentsia emerged and grew in the process of the creation and development of new state and cooperative sector on the basis of social property.[13]

Mongolia's entrance to CMEA, pumped in required capital and technical assistance at a large scale with which Mongolia's pastoral economy was transformed into an agrarian–industrial economy.[14]

From a feudal society it was turned into a socialist one, bypassing the capitalist stage. With Soviet aid, Mongolian society underwent a change in every aspect whether it was economy, politics, religion or social system. With the development of industry, urbanization took place and human resources increased. With the growth of working class, trade unions also emerged. These trade unions played the role of communist colleges, educating people in communist ways. It was these unions who helped the nomadic population in building the new society. Many *arat* associations were formed in order to organise common people in working brigades and train them in communist ideology amid new production schemes. *Arats* were helped in organizing the civic activities on specific pattern through cooperatives. Government encouraged these *arat* cooperatives by giving those funds for building cattle sheds, making hay, transporting loads etc. The schemes were introduced by which family allowances; disability and age old pension was given. Children were given free education in different boarding schools. Workers were provided with long-term credits and material for building private homes. Under these unions veterinary centres, dispensaries, sanatoriums, rest houses, hotels pioneer camps, kindergartens, elementary and secondary schools, recreation and reading rooms, clubs, libraries, radio relay centers, electric power plants were erected and run within the specified planning time frame.

The goal of the communist command economy system was to reduce the disparities and class hierarchy and simultaneously increase efficiency and productivity. However, the same collectives worked in a hierarchy of brigades who decided everything from animal production to marketing.[15] The collectivization succeeded in eliminating the great disparities in income and material possessions of the pre-communist society but gave rise to new classes at work place. Nonetheless, herders were happy with the system as the state employed them and their salaries were guaranteed.[16]

Negdels (associations) became very active to rearrange the existing system of population by sending the herders to many places other than their *torson nutag* (birth place). These *Negdals* changed kin interdependencies; connected groups of different origin and tribal affiliations, who worked more successfully than the members of the same family. To give ample time to the herders, their children were sent to boarding schools from an early age. As the herders were migratory, they were relieved of parenthood obligations by establishing an efficient network of kindergartens and boarding schools which took care of the children, educated them and turned them into well indoctrinated socialist men but simultaneously eroding traditional family patterns and the spirit of parenthood.

The zeal for increasing production, coupled with the abolishing of traditional family structure besides a laxity in sexual relations in the new social order, resulted in the sudden surge in population. Within years the demographic composition and arrangement was all together changed. The illegitimate children and single unwed mothers ceased to be socially rebuked or reprimanded. Majority of such children were taken care of by the state institutions and proved a nursery of indoctrinized socialist subjects, who were loyal to none other than state and its manifestations – be it policies or administrative apparatus. Children born out of wedlock were neither a liability nor economic burden to the family. Infact the children and retired workers used to be the most privileged class in classless societies of all socialist countries.

NOTES

1. Ts.Batkhuu, '*Enteg Sodal*', Indian Studies in Mongolia, Institute of International Studies, Academy of Science and the Center for Indian Studies in Mongolia, no. 4 p. 59.
2. Some times winter last for more than five months. I experienced a light snow fall even in May. During the dzuud (snow storm) time temperature goes so down that the feeling of being alive is lost.
3. *Aimage* is a traditional administrative division in vogue since great Chingiz Khan. In common International connotation Aimage stands for province.
4. Mongolian population, who are the peoples of Mongolia? www-mongol.com>Home> Mongolia
5. Japan granted 1,043,200,000 yen to Mongolia on the ground of emergency caused by a heavy snow storm, which was extended by another 300 million by Prime Minister Yoshiro Mori for further emergency assistance
6. *Ger* is traditional round felt tent of nomads with a central pole. Mongolian population, who are the peoples of Mongolia. www-mongol.com>Home> Mongolia
7. Ts. Batkhuu, "Relations and Cooperation between the Two Capital Cities", *Enteg Sodal* (Indian studies in Mongolia), Institute of International Studies, Academy of Science and Centre for Indian Studies in Mongolian, No. 4, p. 59.
8. During this period many NGOs sprang up who taught people about the basics of democracy and opposed the communist government's (women socialist party) send their volunteers to remote rural images and sums to educate people.
9. In early 80's Mongols had nuclear families. Usually children get a separate Ger from the parents and also a share of herds from both girls and boys parents.
10. Between 16th-17th centuries feudal relations were highly developed Land, the most important tool of the production was the property of the feudal classes. The Mongolian feudal lords controlled huge economic units by utilizing the labour of personal serfs. The personal serfs of the ruling prince had to perform other duties as well without any compensation. Commoners provided their own livestock, manpower and property without compensation. See Sanjdorj M., Manchu Chinese Colonial Rule in Northern Mongolia, (tran) Urgunge Onon, Ulaanbaatar, 1963.
11. During this period Mongolian society turned poor and most people became beggars; the feudal mode of production declined rapidly. Agriculture degenerated and all feudal lama profit got reduced; the impoverished people worked for the feudal lords and could hardly make both ends meet. See Shirendev P., Mongol, Ardiin KhubisgaliinTuukh (History of the Mongolian Peoples Revolution), Ulaanbaatar, 1969.
12. Even foreigners were asked such questions. Many students were thrown out of the universities, sent to remote areas if found to be close to foreign students especially from capitalist countries. However, there was no such bias against Indian students.

13. From 1940 was a stage for Socialism the task of laying the foundation of socialism began with elaboration and realization of sweeping measures designed at transforming agricultural production along socialist principles. Dashdondov, H, India and Mongolia (Experience and Interaction)
14. It was very hard to change the economic strategy, as Mongols believed that the nature would take revenge if they dig the land, as they need to increase the number of their animals rather than their agriculture, as grain cannot be stored for a long time. Chinese were hired for the farming.
15. Swift Jeremy, "Rural Development; The Live Stock Sector," in Keith Griffin (ed), Poverty and the Transition to a Market Economy in Mongolia, Macmillan and St Martins Press, Basingstoke and New York, 1994, p.108.
16. In 1997 some of the informant were not happy with the market economy and longed for the pervious system when life was much easier. They said that they have no money to pay even their apartment rent. Personal interview.

Street Children, Underlying Factors 3

TRANSITION

Street children are a new social phenomenon in Mongolia although the formulation was not exclusive to Mongolia. Infact India, South-east Asia and many underdeveloped countries of Latin America have long experienced it in different versions. However, there is no trace of it in earlier periods of Mongol history. Like many other social evils, the phenomenon was totally absent under communist dispensation. With the collapse of the Soviet Union and dismantling of communist system, a number of social situations typified as social pathology surged forth in all federating units and satellite states woven around communist ideology and command economy. A multiplicity of factors contributed to the emergence and dynamics of many social problems including street children.

Fig. 3.1: Taking care of each other (Courtesy: Journalist Nomi Leh)

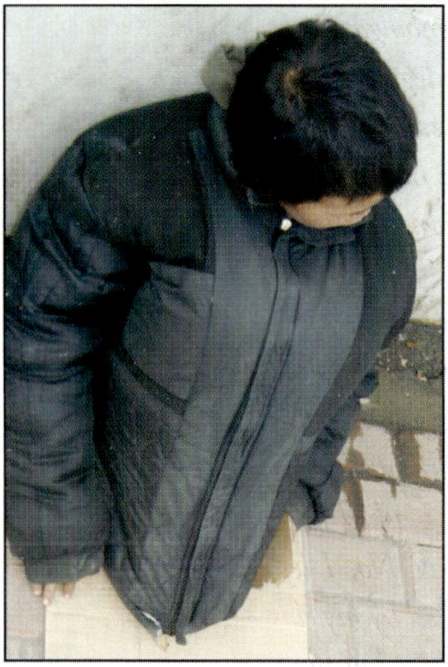

Fig. 3.2: A beggerboy on the central street of Ulaanbaatar (Courtesy: Journalist Nomi Leh)

State and the society were in shock with the new wave of democracy, market economy and otherwise forbidden capitalism. With the limited native resources, melting subsidies and Soviet squeezed aid, the new state apparatus failed to provide any social benefit to its people, which they were used to in the previous system. Failure of social network brought a huge economic pressure on the families. With the result, families broke down and most affected were the children who were left without any care either by their family or state. These abandoned children took shelter in shabby structures on streets and even in underground sewage tunnels in order to protect themselves from the cold and abuse of adults. They spent their nights in sewage pipes, basements and attics of apartment houses and office buildings.

During early years of independence there were countless such children thronging Ulaanbaatar street and its bye lanes. Most of these children, boys and girls are without families and their number is increasing. It is a mixed lot; some of these kids have run away from their homes, some are dropouts from schools and some are just thrown out of the homes by their parents. Society discriminates and maltreats them. These children are denied the access to the basic rights to healthcare, education and psychological wellbeing. They are discarded as drug addicts, prostitutes, beggars and petty thieves. Mongol society in general looks at them as a threat to the society and detests them as a shame. Their illegal activities often land them in detention centers and prisons for long periods, where instead of reformation the criminal tendencies get harden.

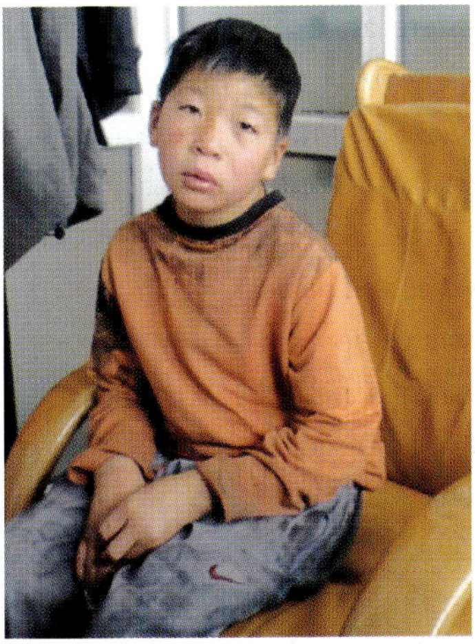

Fig. 3.3: Interview with Erdenbolgan (Photo by Author)

Erdenbolgan is 13-year-old boy, much privileged as he has a shelter though underweight looking much younger than his age with clear bright eyes. He is living in the child centre provided by the "Save Children Fund organization from past two years and center is looking after him. After taking up the street life he usually stays in PC (play game centers or computer centers). As it was working day, I asked him if he is not going to school? No, I left the school as I was bullied by my classmates and beaten by teachers but now I am going to a new school where center has admitted me. This school is good, earlier it was very bad to me, my teachers were also bad to me. I like to study but I cannot read and write yet.

Do you have family? Yes, "My family was bad to me so I do not want to see my parents. My parents know I am in the center. I don't like my father. He always beats me up, as he is always drunk. For two nights I was out in the open street during winter. Sometimes I work and make payment for PC. There are many like me. We play together. They are good to me just like my brothers and sisters. We look after each other and have good understanding. Occasionally we collect bottles and cans together to make some money. Sometimes older akh[1] (brothers) take away our money. They are threatening; however, it is good to stay in PC. How are you living there in PC? Usually the centers are open until ten in the night but the Dargaa (owner) locks us up for night and we like to stay over as we could play whole night. There are many elder kids too, who beat us and take our money but as I like playing games I don't mind getting beaten. Is it free to stay? No, PC take 1900 tugrick[2] from us. It is very warm there. You don't want to return home? Yes sometimes I feel going home but it is nice in the center. I like it here as I could play here and get meals as I cannot get all that in my home. My parents are jobless so they do not care for me being out or in the center. As we have no ger so they too are homeless. As soon as they get one I may return."

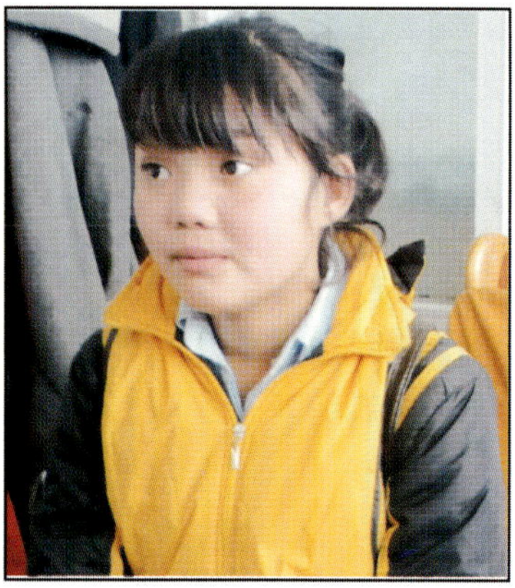

Fig. 3.4: Interview with Oyunzul (Photo by Author)

Oyunzul, often lives on the streets. She is shy and uncomfortable. She is in her teens. When asked why she has chosen this sort of life? She replied, I would be going home soon. She does not have legitimate father. Her mother and grandmother live without a male member. They don't always like to admit that they sleep in the streets, especially teenagers. Oyunzul has a tough life, her mother is an alcoholic and her grandma sells products at the *Sukhbaatar* Square Ulaanbaatar. The children often leave their homes because they have problems at home. They also don't reveal their family addresses lest they may be sent back to their homes, which they do not like. However, care centers convince them that they will not be sent home by force and will be allowed to stay until they agree to return. Oyunzul comes to the center sometimes, but she also visits another center called "*Hugjliin Helhii*". This center is an overnight center. Although the administrative staff of these centres is sympathetic to the children but the centre are not safe for them. Teenagers like Oyunzul are quite vulnerable lot in such centers. They often leave the children to themselves, locking them up in the building.

As per the Manager of the centre, "These children are thieves, trained by adults who use them to make money. It is difficult

> at the center, because often the toys and books disappear. Some of the kids have completed their terms in Juvenile detention centers and therefore, they have been exposed to all sought of abnormal and anti-social activities. People always scold, criticize and abuse them. They've grown up with this kind of treatment from society. It is sometimes a challenge for us to adjust to their abnormal behaviour."
>
> Christina Noble Fund head Mr. Edward Thornton adds that there are kids abandoned by the families and one such 9 year girl was thrown out of her house. Usually kids do not remember their date of birth. She is from *Derkahn*, another metropolitan city. She was gang raped and brought to the ger village from the hospital. Ger villages were constructed by Christian Noble Foundation for such kids and destitute families who did not own a house. In a shock she used to cry first two years but now she is a self-confident girl. She was enrolled in school and is a very brilliant child. Some out fits were made for her so that she does not feel inferior. She prepares for graduation course. There is another girl who was raped by two men and she is very disturbed. Some boys who were brought here from a home school in some American religious sect where they were taught only English. They are Mongols but cannot speak any Mongolian. They have lost their smiles and seem depressed."

It was stated in *Ardiin Erik* on December 15th 2009 that there are many young girls like 9 year old girl who was sexually assaulted and had transmitted the sexual disease, who could not talk to anybody as she did not know about the disease or about the abuse. She was quite unaware to consult a doctor.

Such situations worsened because the transition economy worsened the family conditions whereby kids turned into a burden on household expenditure. In many cases the attitude of the stepfather or alcoholic mother is disturbing so these children prefer to stay back in the computer centers and play games. They also get addicted to these games and lose interest to return their homes, where it is cold and without food. They even steal money to play games. Officials versions state that there are 10 per cent children who return to the society and find some jobs, 20 per cent commit suicide and 40 per cent become criminals.[3]

Some centers allow an overnight stay to the street kids where they are co-habited by street adult also. Because of lack of supervision, there is a typical hierarchy and bossism among inmates. Some children are usually too scared to go to these places. "Save Children Fund" has asked the state to establish a child protection framework. It has also approached the Parliament to make some changes in family law. As per the head of the center, "The state once proposed a project to re-introduce 53 children back into society. The project was shelved at the very beginning because of lack of funds".

Until 1989, the state looked after the welfare of children, whereas during transition the whole mechanism collapsed. Successive measures taken by the administration such as institutionalizing play game centers, identification bureau, counseling centers and legal apparatus lacked coordination which led to a confusing situation. It aggravated the plight of street children instead of their reformation. Lack of coordination among various agencies meant lack of accountability where no unit knew which agency is responsible for what.

The Soviet period was looked as a period of development and progress. Mongolia achieved high development in human resources such as population growth and increase in life expectancy. Adult literacy rose to 93 per cent. Gender equality in every field was exemplary. 98 per cent of women were literate and 86 per cent were in labour force. Virtually the entire population had access to health services, 98 per cent of the pregnant women received prenatal care, 87 per cent of one year old children were immunized against different diseases. Malnutrition was rare and there was an overall improvement in social and economic life.

This progress was not without taking a toll of prevalent social norms of a nomadic society. Rapid industrialization resulted in urbanization with all its associated advantages and disadvantages which during transition was the first causality. The situation in political and economic spheres was rapidly changing and it was very difficult to make structural and institutional adjustments to consolidate them. In early 90's democracy and market economy brought with it inflation, unemployment, widening gap between the rich and poor resulting in lower living standards that shattered the whole socio-economic system of Mongolia. A new professional urban class cut of all links to traditional life style and livestock herding. This class has gone under a tremendous socio-economic stress, as their salaries have diminished and they have lost the purchasing power. In order to maintain their status they have tried to supplement it with alternative sources of income. Many people have taken part time jobs as taxi drivers and petty traders to get money for survival. Some teachers are working as tourist guides; some have opened their own private schools while as doctors have taken jobs as interpreters, engineers as consultants and a marginal number had returned to herding.

PRIVATIZATION

The establishment of new constitution following the democratic revolution has led to the changes in all spheres of Mongolian life. The structural changes in Mongol society led to the functional implications of almost all the institutions. In order to connect Mongol economy to international monetary system, privatization became not only a prerequisite but a norm as well. The privatization and de-collectivization of cultivable land and state property, which started in 1991 turned to be the prime factor affecting the children. With gradual transfer of *Negdel* assets to the members the families were hard hit. Initially most *Negdels* became joint stock companies with some collective ownership of assets and uniform planning at the district level. By 1993 government had privatized some 2440 small enterprises by distributing red and blue vouchers to entire population. The second stage of privatization again through vouchers and cash took place in 1995.[4]

With the privatization, majority of the herders were thrown into an open cut throat competition. In addition, withdrawal of state support caused considerable wealth differentiation among herding households.[5] The large families and single mother families were left to fetch for themselves in open market, for which they were neither ready nor accustomed to.

In order to minimize the gap between the rich and the poor, taxation laws were revised. In rural areas, private livestock varied according to income and market price of the animal products in each household. Although low-income families, old age pensioners and herders with less than 150 heads of livestock were exempted from the income tax, however, these sections failed to cope with the competition in herding and marketing.

The removal of the *Negdel* structure and withdrawal of state support forced the herders to fall back to kinship ties and affiliations for mutual support. Communities like the *neg usnii khun* (people who drink the same water) or *neg nutagiin khun* (people from the same place) of one water source or natal land re-emerged which were long abolished during collectization campaign. People began to cluster together, develop real or fictitious kinship bonds for legitimizing their claim to pasture land on the basis of birth and belonging.

With the privatization many people were left unemployed and those urbanites with rural background had no option but to return to their native places, to resume their old profession as herders. The temptation to own the livestock also created ecological problems, overgrazing of pastures and deforestation. It was typical scenario of counter urbanization. Unfortunately due to repeated *zuud* for past years this segment alongwith some chunks of rural population migrated back to the cities, mostly to Ulaanbaatar, where homeless and without any support, their conditions became vulnerable.[6]

Lack of support from the state and the economic cutbacks affected elderly women and more so the children.

In early 90's many Mongols crossed the border on both Chinese and Russian side. They bought goods with a cheap price and sold at a very high price. The Mongols who bartered these goods became financially very sound. In absence of a viable state apparatus and legal safeguards, coupled with a disbelief in accepted norms, people fell back to illegal mechanisms. A kinship affiliation in Inner Mongolia and Xinxiang was instrumental for a section of society, who got economically benefited. The trend also accelerated shadow economy causing loss to state exchequer, besides leading to unequal distribution of wealth. Mr. Gankhuyag, Director Research Centre of the Mongolian Parliament, wrote in his article, published in Ardiin Erkh:

> "*Ties between natives lie on real relations existent in Mongolian society, relying on the traditions that give rise to a new type of business networking. So we can say that a person with many friends can feel like a grazing animal in vast rolling plain. Mongolians if they want to get some job done they would rather go to their friend and acquaintances who are holding important posts rather than bothering about law and other factors, which could help them, get their jobs done. The bribery, existent in the old order notoriously banned as rear door, corruption and mafia today are all related to each other and have their common source in the society.*"

For Mongols of both sides it was easy to travel either to Chinese Mongolia or Russian Buryat and Khamyk. The Mongols who had access took advantage of the situation and who were not smart enough, were pushed to the lowest ebb.

Lack of experience and technical manpower along with a grave economic recession pushed the vast majority of the rural population towards a self-reliance strategy based on customary livestock rearing practices. It required meagre inputs but simultaneously provided subsistent outputs. The *Negdel* no longer provided animal shelter, veterinary services and transportation as done before and due to this overall production remained much less the same. Herders were not comfortable with the new system and were worried that this might create a class of rich and poor, most of them expressed nostalgia for old days."[7]

According to the European Bank report, Mongolia's GDP grew in recent years but as far as poverty reduction is concerned it has done very little to improve it. "While the incidence of poverty was 36.1 per cent in 2002-03, the latest household survey shows that 35.2 per cent of the population (or 930,000 people) remain below the poverty line. This remains significantly above the MDG target of 18 per cent by 2015. The data also shows that income disparities between rich and poor in urban and rural areas have increased. In urban areas, the reduction was larger (from 30.3 to 26.9 per cent) while in rural areas, the poverty ratio actually increased to 46.6 per cent from 43.4 per cent. This indicates that the population, particularly in rural areas did not benefit enough from economic growth."[8]

Cultural and Educational Decline

At the time of transition Mongolia's literacy rate was among the highest in the world. The literacy rate of 97 per cent in early 1990s dipped slightly during transition years mainly due to a decrease in enrolment to 86.6 per cent in primary education and 71.5 per cent in secondary education in 2001, although it improved and reached 98 per cent in 2007. This recovery in literacy rates despite falling enrolment rates, from 99 per cent in pre-transition years to about 95 per cent in 2007 can be attributed to the development of the non-formal education sector.[9]

Table 3.1: Key Indicators of Poverty in Mongolia

	1990	2000	2005	2006	2015
Poverty Headcounts[5]	36.3 (1995)	35.6 (1998)	36.1 (2002)	32.2	18.0[a]

Source: NSO, 1990-2006

a. SGH Resolution #25-Approval of Mongolia MDGs, 2005

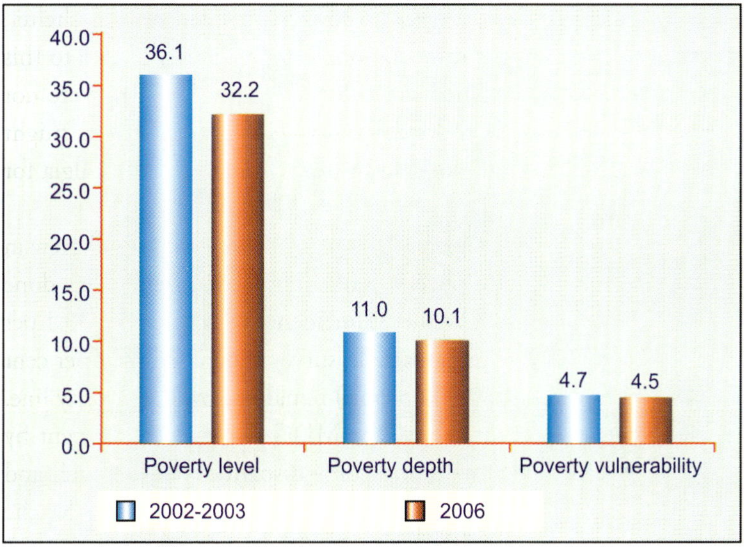

Fig. 3.5: NSO, 2007

As the support and financial aid from Soviet Russia and Central government of Mongolia started shrinking, the whole system of

Table 3.2: Poverty Headcount and Gini Coefficient by Location

	Poverty Level (%)		*Gift Coefficient*	
	2002-2003	*2006*	*2002-2003*	*2006*
National Average	36.1	32.2	0.329	0.380
By location				
Urban	30.3	27.9	0.331	0.386
Ulaanbaatar	27.3	20.4	0.332	0.367
Almag centers	33.9	36.1	0.324	0.389
Rural	43.4	37.0	0.313	0.360
By region				
Western	51.1	38.7	0.306	0.342
Hartgai	38.7	37.7	0.320	0.354
Central	34.4	34.0	0.314	0.393
Eastern	34.5	36.5	0.317	0.399
Ulaanbaatar	27.3	20.4	0.332	0.367

Source: NSO "Household Income, Expenditure Survey" 2006.
NSO, Household Income, Living Standard Measurement Survey, 2002-2003.
NSO, National Statistical Bulletin, 2006.

Table 3.3: Number of Educational Institutions/at the beginning of the academic year, September

	1960	1970	1980	1990	1991	1992	1993	1994	1995	1996
Total	490	813	954	928	782	841	762	819	856	930
General educational school	419	503	571	634	643	679	663	659	664	658
Institutions	22	52	69	84	79	88	89	104	93	113
of which: private	—	—	—	—	—	9	25	31	41	51
General educational school for working persons.	49	258	314	210	60	74	10	56	99	159

Table 3.4: Number of Teachers /thous./

	1960	1970	1980	1990	1991	1992	1993	1994	1995	1996
Teachers - total	4,6	10.1	17,4	25, 2	24,2	22,9	22, 7	22, 5	22, 9	24,1
general educational school	3,8	8.7	13,9	20,6	20,5	19,4	19,2	19,1	19,4	20,1
professional institutions	0,8	1.4	3,5	4,6	3,7	3.5	3,5	3,4	3,5	4,0

Table 3.5: Number of Pupils and Students in Educational Institutions /at the beginning of the academic year, thous./

	1960	1970	1980	1990	1991	1992	1993	1994	1995	1996
Total	131,0	276, 0	458, 4	516.2	467,5	426,7	409,4	425,2	456,5	482,7
General educational schools	107,2	230.4	372,1	440,9	411,7	384,0	370.3	381.2	403,8	418,3
Primary vocational training institutions	—	10,6	22,1	29,1	19,3	11,5	8,3	7,5	8,0	11,3
Special secondary institutions*	8.8	11, 1	18,7	18,5	15,8	10.9	5,8	5,9	5,6	3,7
Higher institutions*	6,9	8, 4	23,2	17,3	17,5	17,5	24,2	27,9	33,7	40,4
General educ. schools for working people	8,1	15.5	22,3	10,4	3.2	2,8	0,8	2.7	5,4	9, 0

* Included students studied abroad.

Source: Mongolian Economy and Society in 1996, State Statistical Office of Mongolia, Ulaanbaatar, 1997.

healthcare and education collapsed. Economic recession hit the families and children as their parents could not afford to provide them with the basic needs. According to the UNDP Human Development Report from 1992-1998, government expenditure on health and education dropped from 16.2 per cent to 14 per cent.[10]

The percentage decrease in education was higher than the decline in GDP or total public expenditure. The basic educational system was in the state of crisis with enrolment declining, dropout rate rising and teachers opting for new jobs. Not only in the *Aimag*s but also in urban areas children were not registered, schools were deserted and a few of them were overcrowded. Without the state help poor parents could not afford basic school needs.

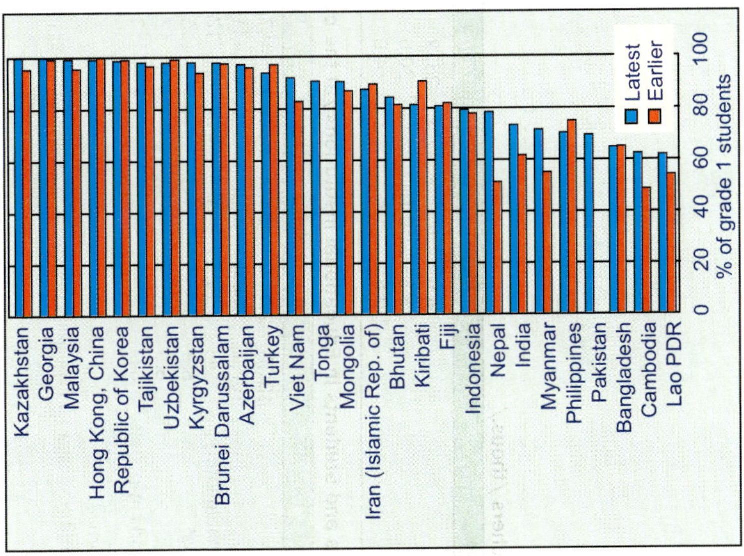

Fig. 3.6: Proportion of Primary Students Reaching Grade 5 Asia and the Pacific, 1999-2006[12]

The Socialist period in Mongolia was characterized by extremely high gross enrolment rates. By the year 1988, over 70,500 children attended 718 kindergartens, and there were 604 general secondary schools with 430,500 pupils. In 1989, there were 98 per cent in primary schools and 85 per cent in secondary schools.[11]

EDUCATION IN MONGOLIA

As compared to other developing countries, Mongolia stood relatively high in terms of primary education. However, influenced by the post 1990 transition in governance that resulted in political confusion and social reforms, the decrease in primary education has been alarming.

Fig. 3.7: Helping the Family (Courtesy: Journalist Nomi Leh)

The (Table 3.6) shows the declining net enrolment ratio in primary education over the years from 1999-2006. According to the National Report, during academic years of 2005-2006, the proportion of 1-5 grade dropouts represented 83.2 per cent, indicating two out of three students dropping out from primary schools.[14] As the data sheet shows about 40 per cent of the 2.6 million population being under age 15, the issue of basic education involved a considerable portion of the nation affecting the future of Mongolia.

Table 3.6: Primary Education Prevalence[13]

	1990	*2000*	*2005*	*2006*	*2015*
Net enrolment ratio in primary education	95.9 (1997)	95.0	93.3	91.4	100.0[a]
Proportion of pupils starting grade 1 who reach grade 5	91.0	83.6	101.2	86.8	100.0[a]
Literacy rate among 15-24 age group	99.0	97.7	97.7 (2000)	97.7 (2000)	100.0[a]

Source: NSO, 2006.

a. SGH Resolution #25 - Approval of Mongolia MDGs, 2005.

After the livestock sector was privatized, the herders needed help and labour for tending their stock. The students especially boys were compelled to leave schools to help their families curtailing their chance to get education. A significant correlation is manifested in livestock privatization and dropout rate.

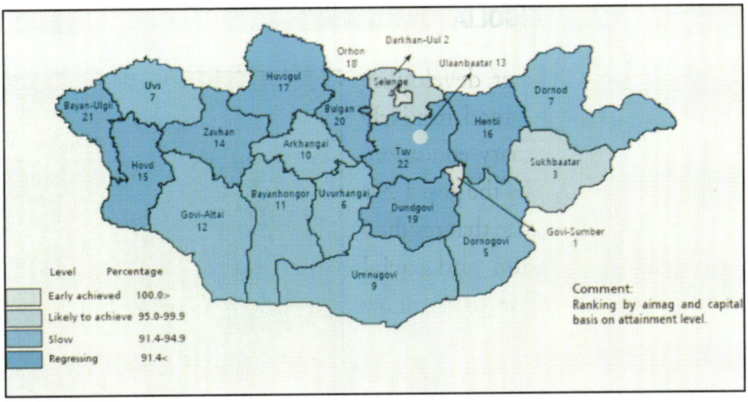

Source: NCO, 2006.

Fig. 3.8: Universal Primary Education Target, by Aimag, 2006

Regional Comparison indicates that most of the regions in Mongolia largely present either "slow" or "regressing" levels, demonstrating overall deficits that plague the country as a whole. However, there is marked difference on rural urban continuum, with the exception of dropouts being lower in Ulaanbaatar suggesting that the dropout phenomenon is more common among the rural areas.

The study reveals that cattle breeding on privatization pattern emerged as the primary factor for the dropout rate in the schools, specifically in rural areas.[15] Considering the herding period which is seasonal, therefore, refunding for dropout programmes may be necessary to increase the retention ability in primary education especially among those affected by income-earning activities.

Fig. 3.9: Leaning on each other (Courtesy: Journalist Nomi Leh)

Social-Regression

According to the latest estimates from the National Statistical Office, the number of children in the labour force in Mongolia is estimated at 43,158 (6.9 per cent of children). The ILO office indicated that child labour is not an issue in Mongolia.

In rural areas, children help in household work and herding occasionally. However, in most cases herders help is seasonal i.e. only a few weeks a year, otherwise parents tend to give priority to children's education. The school participation rate is actually rising and improving and the education level is reasonably high in Mongolia.

Fig. 3.10: Left without Care (Courtesy: Journalist Nomi Leh)

The child labour differs from rural and urban areas. In the rural areas children are engaged in tending livestock, collecting animal dung for fuel, making hay fanes, fetching water etc. The boys do this work mostly and the girls are involved in domestic help such as making milk products. Whereas in urban areas these kids are engaged in shoe shining, car washing, selling food items etc. It is reported that coal and old mining industry engage children of 5 to 17 years of age group.[16] However, there are claims and counterclaims with regard to the chronic nature of the problem such as long working hours of the parents to meet out household expenditure and other phenomenon.

As parents have to be out of home, children are left alone in the house. This affects the children's psychological development who have nobody to guide or support. According to the child identification centre, in such cases children enjoy maximum freedom but share a few responsibilities. Currently children have 32 rights but only 6 responsibilities. Children have little understanding of what are their rights and corresponding responsibilities.

Ardiin Erkh May 10th 1994, report that the children who live inside the trains are 50,000; the children who live on their own by

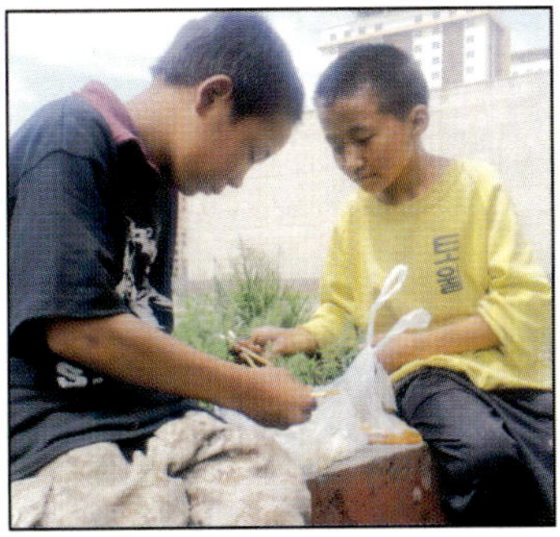

Fig. 3.11: Art of Living and Sharing (Photo by Author)

selling food items are around 10,000 and the number of children with legal label of pick pockets and pity thieves is about 20,000. UNICEF spent 130,000 US dollars for its three year project to facilitate their reform. Many voluntary workers were recruited to help and contribute. In 1994, the documentary film "Forgotten Future", depicting children's plight was made by some journalist but the Government refused to telecast it. The government did not want to make the reality public as it was felt the problem was a shame for the image of the country at the international level.[17]

The most serious problem is alcoholism against which Mongolian government is fighting since ages.[18] It was mentioned in the *Mongol Messenger* – a National daily, in 1995 that to enter the university most popular weapon to bribe the teacher was alcohol.[19] Alcoholism eats up family expenditure, destroys healthy family environs and indirectly impacts personality development of the child. Another chronic problem is rampant corruption in every walk of Mongol life. The UN Convention on Anti-Corruption was ratified by Mongolia. They created a legal framework for fighting corruption. An Anti-Corruption Agency is responsible for investigating corruption cases. Corruption remains a major problem and more tangible practical results in combating corruption are needed. It is not accidental that an anti-corruption ticket on which Elbegdorj campaigned during the latest presidential election appealed to large segments of the electorate.[20]

DISINTEGRATION OF FAMILIES

In nomadic social system of Mongolia, a woman enjoyed maximum freedom and was not bound by hard and fast rules of marital relationship. She was free to interact with people of opposite sex, demonstrating her independent personality. The children born out of illegal relationships (be it with the Russian, Chinese, Japanese or Korean) used to be a class by themselves with distinct identity these children are called Erliiz[21] and have confusing parentage. This tendency solidified during socialist rule, turned into a cherished norm with regard to increasing population of Mongolia.

Fig. 3.12: Working for Survival: A Boy in a Workshop

(Courtesy: Journalist Nomi Leh)

In the socialist period women were encouraged to have as many children as possible to increase population. The more children meant equal pay with men, maternity allowances, free medical health, Glorious Mother title, allotment of a summer house, free education and many other such facilities. It was not necessary to have a legal marriage bond but with the collapse of planned economy, state was unable to provide these "Glorious Mothers" any sort of financial help.[22] Unable to feed large families, economic difficulties forced children out of homes to streets for survival.

In many families such children became the bread winners as many of them were forced to leave schools and work even in very hazardous conditions. Since the whole economic system collapsed, government had to shut down boarding schools. Children from rural areas had to return to their native places or do petty jobs on the streets.

Adultery and promiscuity in Mongolia have a long tradition without any appended taboo or social disapproval. The relationship is socially tolerated provided certain norms are observed. The most important is to uphold, at least publicly, the marital bond which invariably results in neither side acknowledging paternity. Mongol scholars suggest that this cultural pattern in a small isolated population makes it possible for cousins and half siblings to mate, indirectly contributing to genetic abnormalities. Another contributing factor was the non-availability of contraceptives during the socialist period as the state encouraged the fast growth of population.[23]

The large number of single mothers is connected with this tradition of sexual bond. The number of these single headed households was 65,000 in 1989 according to some estimates which increased to 85,000 in 1991. Despite social approval, a change in the attitude is seen as many Mongolians express concern with regard to the illegitimate births, which for them is moral collapse of Mongolian society.[24]

In early 90's these single mothers were terminated from their jobs for survival, they ended up begging and making a living by entering into the flesh trade. The Mongolian men do not have good opinion about this section of population. They are of the opinion that most of the foreigners develop illegal relations with such women and it is national shame.[25]

Yet another problem is migration of men and women to the cities in search of new economic opportunities. Globalization aggravated the problem when many professionals and technical hands both men and women voluntarily migrated to work or study abroad never to return back.[26]

REGIONAL MIGRATION OF MONGOL POPULATION[27]

Women and children are left alone in the countryside without the help of men folk or Negdel. These single women have to look after the house, children and herds and marketing of their herds.[28] Herding season is the time which for herdsmen and women provide ample opportunity for sexual intercourse. During this period young lads, soldiers and strangers pour into the countryside to help and have fun. In urban areas girls with lower education and low income fell to flesh trade to earn quick easy money.[29]

Table 3.7

	Inbound	Outbound	Change	Inbound	Outbound	Change
Western	612	9,539	–8,927	2,318	8,137	–5,819
Hangai	3,468	10,843	–7,375	5,743	10,259	–4,516
Central	6,734	14,163	–7,429	9,449	13,936	–4,487
Eastern	644	4,171	–3,527	1,872	4,371	–2,499
Ulaanbaatar	30,207	2,949	27,258	25,877	8,556	17,321
Total	**41,665**	**41,665**		**45,259**	**45,259**	

Source: NSO (2007) National Statistical Bulletin-2006, UB.

DE-VALUATION OF FAMILY NORMS

It is another dimension of the problem to seriously contemplate upon. During the socialist period both sexes were required to render active service in offices, factories, farms and stores thus helping the family in economic endeavours. They were provided equal opportunities in socio-economic development. After the collapse of the socialist system, a section of men folk were relieved off by the armed forces services and re-deployed at such jobs which customarily were the domain of womenfolk. In such situations women hitherto kept busy in productive jobs were rendered unemployed. The deprived womenfolk took to heavy drinking and showed least interest in keeping household intact, gradually disharmony developed and the families disintegrated.

Alienation and disintegration allowed flush trade to be taken as an easy option which made inroads into the contemporary Mongolian society. Added to it there is evidence of registered cases with the police about the children aged 15 to 17 who were forced to become sex workers. According to the police department the number of sex workers is less than 200 who are registered with the police, but it is very difficult to figure out real number as official statistics are likely grossly understated. These are the sensitive issues. The police – flesh trade nexus further complicates the phenomenon resulting in a few registered cases so as not to attract attention of legal institutions. Although children are the victims but they are not treated as victims.

Mongolia has become a hub for foreigners to seek inexpensive Mongolian young women. The factor leading such underage girls to flesh trade are related to their poverty, low standard of living, and domestic violence. The other attraction for such young girls is the high price offered by their clients. The foreigners seek these virgins as there are far less chances of contracting sexual diseases such as HIV and STDs.

Girl child is consumed in pornography market, for Mongol and non-Mongol customers. Unfortunately unmindful of its consequences the sex workers suffer from sexually transmitted infectious diseases like VD, UTT, and above all AIDS due to the lack of contraceptives. Unwed sex workers abandon their children on streets and after some time the female folk find her place again in the flesh trade market. It proves a breeding pool of constant supply of sex workers. Some NGOs provide life saving skill training to working and street children groups in order to make them aware and save them from HIV/AIDS and sexually transmitted diseases, considering the high risk environment these children are exposed to. *Ardiin Erkh* reported that among the 841 children surveyed, there are 36 types of diseases diagnosed among. Tuberculoses used to be the illness prevalent among older people only, now it was found among the children of 13 to 15 years of age group.

The internal trafficking is another dimension and the involvement of underage girls in flesh trade is increasing in large urbancentres like Ulaanbaatar, *Darkhan-Uul aimag, Darkhan, Orkhon aimag, Eredenet, Selenge aimag, Dornod aimag*, and *Zamiin Uud* for varied reasons. South Korean, Japanese, Swiss, Hungarian sex mafias are said to be connected to trafficking through fraudulent marriages. Most often the grooms are older than the prospective brides.[30]

According to a survey conducted by Elimination of Child Pornography and Child Prostitution and Trafficking (ECPAT) in 2004, the girls who were detained as sex workers were aged between 13-18 years. Furthermore, two-third was the children who had run away from home living on the streets and not enrolled at school.[31]

This is not the case only with the street children, according to the National Health Statistics, the incidence of TB accounted for 10.6 per cent of all the communicable diseases reported in 2007.[32]

The table below shows the details of incidences, prevalence, death rates and percentage of TB case diagnosed and treated with international standard.[33]

Table 3.8

	1990	2000	2005	2006	2015
New incidences of TB (per 100,000 population)	79.0[a]	124.8[a] 125.0[b]	177.4[a]	185.3[a]	100.0[b]
Prevalence of tuberculosis (per 100,000 population)	435.5[a]	60.0[a]	91.2[a]	84.8[a]	–
Death rates associated with tuberculosis (per 100,000 population)	4.8[a] 4.9[b]	3.2[a]	3.4[a]	2.9[a]	0.0[b]
Percentage of TB cases diagnosed and treated with international standard diagnostic and treatment methods	31.4[a] (1994)	80.9[a] 100.0[b]	79.0[a]	82.1[a]	100.0[b]

Source: a. NSO, Statistical Bulletin 2006.

b. 5GH Resolution #25 Approval of Mongolia MDGs, 2005.

LEVEL OF NEW INCIDENTS OF TB BY *AIMAGS*[34]

These children are prone to difficulties; are shy, depressed and lack self confidence. Access to basic services is severely limited among

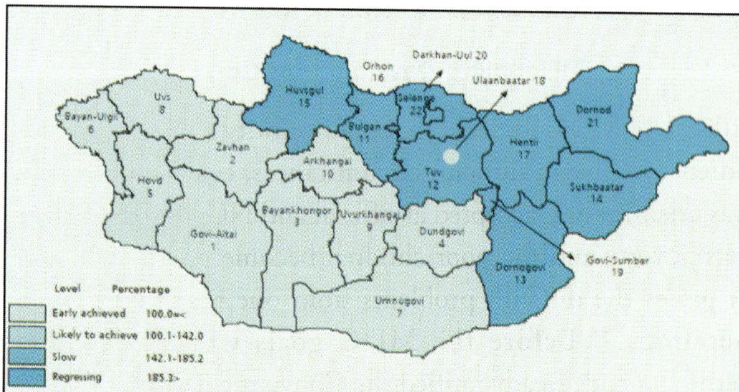

Comment: Ranking by aimag and capital basis on attainment level.

Source: NCO, 2006.

Fig. 3.13

Street and working children, and are particularly prone to the negative impacts of poverty that deny them opportunities to personality development and to live healthy and fruitful lives.

UNICEF report of 2001 states that these children "are more likely to have learning difficulties, prone to drop out of school, develop tendency to resort to drugs and crime. They are likely to be out of work, to become pregnant at an early age and adopt a lifestyle that perpetuates poverty and a disadvantage into succeeding generations."[35]

Fig. 3.14: United Nations MDG's for Mongolia Chair of the Mongolian MDG's Ms. Sanjasureniing Oyun[36] (Photo by Author)

MEASURE FOR REHABILITATION OF STREET CHILDREN

United Nations Millennium Development Goals

In 2002 UN MDG declared that their priority is to rehabilitate street children who live in difficult circumstances, especially in Mongolia. It was unanimously accepted at official and NGO levels that poverty begets poverty and the poor children become poor adults which in turn passes the difficult problems from one generation to another generation."[37] Before the MDG goals were set, Mongolian government had already ratified the Convention on the Rights of the Child in 1990. According to MDG Report of 2007, emphasis was laid on challenging goals of concerned areas related to a high rate of poverty reversing, the spread of tuberculosis, net enrolment rate in

Annex 2: Evaluation and Trend Analysis in Implementation of MDGs

Goals/Targets/Indicators		Baseline	Observed			Target	Gap in years'	Performance
		1990	2000	2005	2006	2015		
GOAL 1	**Reduce Poverty and Hunger**							
TARGET 1	Poverty Headcounts	36.30	35.60	36.10	32.20	18.00	30	Slow
TARGET 2	Prevalence of Underweight children	12.00	12.70	6.30	...	0	8	Likely to achieve
TARGET 3	Develop and implement strategies aimed at creating favorable and productive workplace for youth. Create jobs through increased opportunity to utilize land, simplified rules for small and medium businesses, greater access to credit for unemployed citizens	...	...	...	...	...	...	...
TARGET 4	Reduce negative impact of migration and urbanization, protect rights of migrants, create legal protections, develop systems for provision of jobs, housing, health, education, culture and other social services	...		...	...	...	...	
GOAL 2	**Achieve Universal Primary Education**							
TARGET 5	Provide primary education to all girls and boys by 2015							
	Net enrolment ratio in primary education	95.90	95.00	93.30	91.40	100.00	17	Regressed
	Proportion of pupils starting grade 1 who reach grade 5	91.00	83.60	101.20	86.80	100.00	18	Regressed
	Literacy rate among 15-24 age group	99.00	97.70	...	...	100.00		Regressed

Contd.…

Contd....

Goals/Targets/Indicators		Baseline 1990	Observed 2000	Observed 2005	Observed 2006	Target 2015	Gap in years'	Performance
GOAL 3	**Promote Gender Equality and Empower Women**							
TARGET 6	Eliminate gender disparity in primary and secondary education by 2005 and in all levels of education no later than 2015							
	Ratio of girls to boys in primary education	1.03	1.01	0.98	0.98	1.00	12	Likely to achieve
	Ratio of girls to boys in secondary education	1.33	1.20	1.11	1.03	1.00	...	Achieved
	Ratio of female to male students in higher education institutions		1.72	1.53	1.53	1.00	20	Slow
	Proportion of women in the population engaged in wage employment in non-agriculture sectors	51.10	50.40	53.10	53.90	50.00	22	Regressed
	Percentage of women elected to national parliament	24.90	11.80	6.6	...	30.00	95	Regressed
	Percentage of women candidates in parliamentary election	7.70	10.90	13.7	...	35.00	30	Likely to achieve

Contd....

Contd.…

Goals/Targets/Indicators		Baseline	Observed			Target	Gap in years'	Perfor-mance
		1990	2000	2005	2006	2015		
GOAL 4	**Reduce Child Mortality**							
TARGET 7	Reduce by two-thirds, between 1990 and 2015, the under-five mortality rate							
	Under-five mortality rate (per 1000 live births)	88.80	44.50	26 00	2120	29.20	…	Achieved
	Infant mortality rate (per 1000 live births)	64.40	12.80	20.70	19.10	22.00		Achieved
	Percentage of children covered by immunization against measles	82.30[9']	92.40	97.50	98.90	96.00		Achieved
GOAL 5	**Improve Maternal Health**							
TAR6FT 8	Provide access to all individuals of appropriate age to required reproductive health service and reduce by three-quarters, between 1990 and 2015, the maternal mortality ratio							
	Maternal mortality rate (per 100,000 thousand live births)	121.6	166.30	92 70	67.20	50.00	1	Likely to achieve

primary education, enhancement of gender equality and environmental sustainability.[38]

PROGRESS BY GOAL[39]

In 2003, Mongolian Government with the support of World Bank and International Monetary Fund started to implement the MDG to reduce the poverty. The name of this new strategy was given "Economic Growth Support and Poverty Reduction Strategy" EGSPRS.[40] New modern tools for pasture utilisation were given to herder families. In order to help herders with animal related infectious diseases, opportunities were created for the early diagnosis.

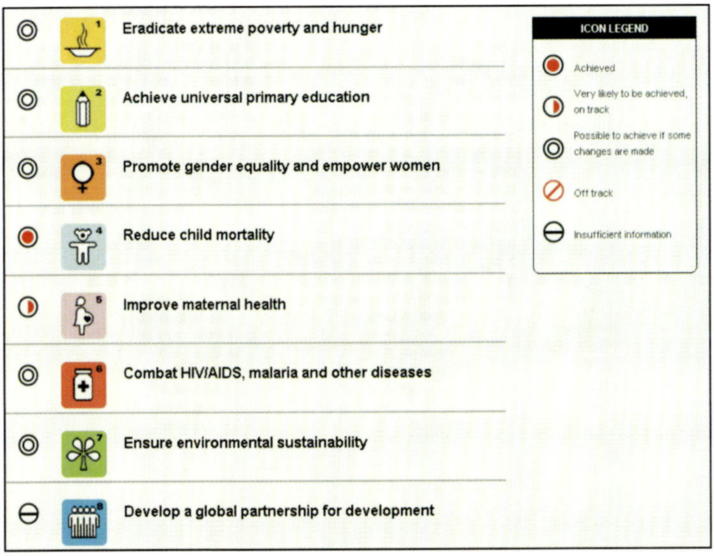

Fig. 3.15: Progress by Goal: Current status in accordance with national Government reporting

On education sector to make life easy for herders, opportunities were provided to children to attend schools, mobile kindergartens and summer school camps besides, old schools were renovated.[41]

However, despite such efforts, the overall MDG progress in Mongolia is considerably slow demonstrating, "unsatisfactory performance and weak coordination of policies and measures aimed at implementation."[42] While over 50 per cent of target indicators show positive outcome, rest of the targets (40 per cent) still require improved policy formation and institutional coordination, calling for much intensified implementation. Yet, due to lack of established nationwide MDG monitoring system, the availability of accurate statistics hinders linking policy priorities with appropriate resource allocation especially to the most needy and vulnerable population.[43] There is an urgency to address issues with a better approach. Multiple target indicator of MDG are to be revised in order to bridge the gap of data disparity to promote inclusive growth.

In order to improve the quality of social welfare system social welfare fund was increased by 20 per cent in 2003 and 2004.[44] In 2008, Mongolia was also affected by the global economic recession and it had very negative impact on the National Action Plan policies for 2008 to 2012. Social welfare programmes suffered due to squeeze in the flow of funds, adversely hitting low income families.[45] Unemployment seemed to be underestimated in the official statistics at 3.3 per cent in 2008, but the real unemployment rate is estimated at 13.1 per cent according to the unofficial sources. Unemployment is higher in urban areas (18.7 per cent) than rural areas (10.0 per cent). However, as wage levels are significantly higher in urban areas and poverty ratio is lower, low-income households still tend to move to urban areas.[46]

Rehabilitation of Street Children by the Government

Mongolian government in collaboration with NGOs has drawn projects to help the destitute children. In the light of "Convention on the Rights of Children," "A World Fit for the Children" and recommendation of Ministerial Staff in East Asia and Pacific Region, with due consideration to Millennium Declaration, the state is seriously trying to improve the conditions of the street children in Mongolia. It was stated that government would give special priority to the convention dealing with the "protection of mothers, combating discrimination in education, voluntary marriage, age limits for marriage, proper registration of marriage, and other international legal documents relating to the protection of the rights of children."[47]

Rehabilitation of children figures among several measures taken by the government to repair the economy and rebuild social system. In December 1996, Prime Minister of Mongolia made an emergency call for providing shelter to such children. Various organizations came forward to lend their helping hand in the rehabilitation of this unfortunate lot. Orphanage centres were increased, foster programmes established, and poor and needy children were provided with free study material, textbooks, uniforms and meals. In 1990, "*Itgel*" (Hope) centre was established where mostly orphans and the children who are maltreated either by their stepfathers or stepmothers are placed. It was found that some of the children adjusted to the atmosphere of the centre but others do not and run away because they are used to street life. The new system brought new opportunities besides bringing a tremendous social and economic pressure on common people. Many social organizations came forward to support and rehabilitate these children by providing those jobs and encouraged them to study besides doing work. To be more productive these children were given vocational training in order to enable them to acquire skills to secure jobs at state and private level. Financial difficulties curtail optional alternatives despite all available measures it became very difficult to eradicate this social evil.

Present field investigation reveals that progress in this direction has been considerable despite financial constraints and lack of infrastructure. A comprehensive approach is required addressing needs of the children born into marginalized families. As street children are a social and economic issue, the government and NGOs working in coordination are engaged in minimizing the number of street children on the roads in the first instance. Compared to mid-90's, the situation has changed. The number of street children on the streets has declined owing to the efforts of social service centres, operated both by governmental and non-governmental organizations. According to

Christina Noble head, "the number has decreased enormously partially because of *ger* houses and educating centres that keep them on vocational programmes and get them jobs."[48]

Officially it was stated that the number of the street children in the beginning of early 90's was 30,000. In 1995 and 1996 the number was stated to be 60,000 including 2,000 working children in the market.

The data on child protection from governmental and non-governmental agencies revealed that:

- 1,186 children were placed in Care centres.
- The number of disabled children increased slightly from 8,725 in 2000 to 8,811 in 2005.
- In 2004, 5,429-orphans were registered compared to 4,312 in 2000.
- It is estimated that 10.1 per cent (68,580) children nationwide are engaged in economic activities of which 65 per cent are boys and nearly a fourth do not attend school.

Fig. 3.16: Centre for street children Save the Children Fund (Photo by Author) (Due to swine flu children wear masks provided by the centre)

- 65 per cent of 1,871 children engaged in hazardous forms of child labour are boys who mainly work in the mining sector.

- The number of children lost during migration, abandoned, runaway from dis-functional homes or orphaned were 4,000 in 1990s, and 75 per cent lived in Ulaanbaatar. Number of underage girls engaged in commercial sex trade increased by 82 per cent from 38 in 2001 to 215 in 2005 while children in conflict with the law showed a 22 per cent decline from 1,703 in 2002 to 1,332 in 2005."[49]

Fig. 3.17: Living together in Children's Identification Center, Ulaanbaatar (Photo by Author)

Mr. *Purevhoshuuch,* an official of Children Address Identification Centre believes that Ulaanbaatar is divided into nine districts, *Baganuur, Bagakhangai, Bayangol, Bayanzurikh, Chingeltei, Khaanuul, Nalaikh, Songino khairkhan* and *Sukhbaatar*. Out of the nine *Bayangol* and *Bayanzuri kh* contain majority of street children. *Bayangol* district has 20 Orphanage Centers with children as small as 0-3 years old. These centres house over a hundred children and are sometimes overcrowded.

Besides, Orphanage centres, there are now 45 children's care centres. Five of them are run by the state and receive state funding whereas the remaining are mainly run by International organizations and private foundations with financial and technical support. They have a credit system based on age, social and education ratings. Most of these places are affiliated to some type of religious institution.[50]

There are also overnight centres that are financed by foreign organizations. Despite providing food and shelter they lack family atmosphere, comments head of an identification centre. When children come in the morning into these centres, they are provided with breakfast and lunch. They are also given some pocket money and asked to come back again. These children use the money to play PC (computer) games. These practices make children used to receiving charity. Instead of being motivated to help out with domestic chores these children get used to easy money. A significant section of respondents are of the opinion that these children should be enrolled in military schools where they could get education, a specialized field and be imbued with patriotic feelings. However, the children's rights, law of the land and the society prevent such forms of education from being put into practice.

Christina Noble operates health care program in the modern child hospitals where there is a clinic that opens every day and is staffed by two doctors and a nurse. They sponsor children and their relatives. The street children as well as the *ger* children get the prescription and the medicines free of cost as the bills are paid by organizations. Mobile night clinics equipped with an ambulance and expert medical team treat street children three nights a week in summer and four nights in winter around the outskirts of Ulaanbaatar but majority of them live in city centres.

NOTES

1. *akh* usually is elder brother but in Mongolia they don't address by name so the male person who is elder is called *akh* or female is called *ekche* and younger both male and female is *duu*.
2. Equivalent to 1.33 US $.
3. *Ardiin Erkh* 2009, 15th December.
4. Mongolian Messenger, October 4th, 1995.

5. Bruun. O. and O. Odgoard, "A Society and Economy in Transition" in Bruun. O. (ed), Mongolian in Transition, Curzon Press, 1996, pp. 65-89.
6. The Ger area Sharkhad is populated with these urban poor families. High costs of housing, fuel and staple food is adversely affecting their appalling living conditions.
7. Goldstein, M.C. and C. M. Beall, The Changing World of Mongolia's Nomads, University of California Press, Berkely, 1994, pp. 103-105.
8. European Bank for reconstruction and development strategy for Mongolia, Bank Report, October 2009.
9. Education Financial Planning in Asia: Implementing Medium Term Expenditure Frame Works Mongolia, Sukhumvit Rd., Prakanong Bangkok Thailand.
10. Living Standards Measurement Survey, National Statistics Office/UNDP, 1998.
11. Mongolia: Investment Environment and Opportunities, Ulaanbaatar, 1996, p. 26.
12. Statistical Yearbook for Asia and the Pacific, (2008) Educational Outcomes, http://www.unescap.org/STAT/data/syb2008/13-Educational-outcomes.pdf
13. UNDP (n.d). Mongolia (2007), National Report.
14. UNDP (n.d). Mongolia (2007), National Report.
15. Kishigbuyan, D. and Bundii, R., School Dropouts in Mongolia. Mid-Decade Review of Progress Towards Education, United Nations Educational, Scientific, and Cultural Organization,1996, http://www.eric.ed.gov:80/ERICDocs/data/ericdocs2sql/content_storage_01/0000019b/80/17/25/cc.pdf
16. NCHR, The Worst Form of Child Labourin Mongolia, Study Report, Ulaanbaatar, 2008.
17. The documentary was telecasted on NHK (Japan National Broadcasting) with the title "Manhole Children" in 2009. The script of the documentary is knitted around one girl and two boys living together on streets. The depiction of strained relationships, poverty and suffering are appalling.
18. When the author was in Mongolia, way back in 80s even during the daytime men in a drunken state fell down on the streets. Mongols always blamed Russians for their vodka drinks and now they are blaming Chinese. Chinese lifestyle and mannerism is making serious inroads in Mongol culture. Mongol students studying in Japan have serious reservations about Chinese men marrying Mongol girls. Instead they prefer Japanese to grooms of their Mongol sisters and daughter, personal interview.
19. Alcohol (Changiz vodka) is also the favorite souvenir a Mongol exchange student brings to the teachers in other countries where alcohol is a culture like Japan, for grades and jobs.
20. European Bank for Reconstruction and Development Strategy for Mongolia as approved by the Board of Directors meeting 21 October, 2009.
21. Some Foreigners who have illegal children with Mongolian women have started giving the children their family name. for instance the Japanese who cohabit with Mongolian women without marriage have given such children their parental name, personal interview.

22. Globalization, particularly for transitional countries, can fracture local communities and rearrange social order, often leaving women with the responsibility for their own and their children's survival. That is what is happening in Mongolia now. Helen Jones, "Working Together: Local and Global Imperatives for Women in Mongolia", *Asian Europe Journal*, Vol. 4, Issue 3, 2006, pp. 417-430.
23. Uradyn E. Bulag, Nationalism and Hybridity in Mongolia, Clarendon Oxford, 1998 p. 108.
24. Ibid, p. 110.
25. It seems that Mongolian men are convinced that their women are notoriously known to foreigners as '*zeer*' antelopes, which suggests that foreigners come to Mongolia not only on safari, but also hunt for women game. Mongolian women are an easy prey, instigating foreigners for molestation and rape. See Uradyn. E. Bulag, Nationalism and Hybridity in Mongolia, Clarendon Oxford, 1998.
26. Globalization is also transporting the social evil to other countries. This is like a parasite, which is eating the morals of the countries where some of these students and professionals in search of good life break the social norms of the country. They get involved in sex rackets and extra marital affairs. In such cases the ultimate sufferer is mother and child.
27. UNDP (n.d). Mongolia (2007) National Report.
28. Skapa, B., and F. A. Benwell, "Women and Poverty During the Transition", in (ed) Mongolia in Transition, Curzon Press, 1996, pp. 135-146.
29. Some luxurious hotels have become havens for street girls, seeking to get richer through foreign customers from whom they can earn 80 to 200 US dollars a night and sometimes only 10 dollar, personal interview.
30. Human trafficking.org/Mongolia.
31. Situation Analysis of Children and Women in Mongolia, UNICEF-Mongolia, Ulaanbaatar, 2007, p. 66.
32. Ministry of Health, (2008), Mongolia Health Informatin System: Assessment Report, http://www.who.int/healthmetrics/library/countries/hmn_mng_hisassessment.pdf.
33. UNDP (n.d). Mongolia (2007) National Report.
34. Ministry of Health. (2008). Mongolia Health Informatin System: Assessment Report. http://www.who.int/healthmetrics/library/countries/hmn_mng_hisassessment.pdf.
35. UNICEF Report 2001.
36. Ms Sanjaasuren Oyun is presently Minister of Nature, Environment and Green Development, Former Foreign Minister of Mongolia.
37. UNICEF (n.d), (2002), Every Child Has the Right to Healthy Growth, Health and nutrition, http;//www.unicef.org/Mongolia/UNICEF_factsheet_eng.pdf.
38. UNDP (n.d). Mongolia (2007) National Report.
39. UNDP (n.d). Mongolia. (2007). MDG Progress.
40. With this policy Government was able to provide the effective services to the Poor. Projects like Sustainable Livelihoods Project with USD 18.6 million,

Sustainable Reduction of Rural Poverty Project with USD 16.6 million for agricultural development and development for the poor household income growth were implemented in many aimages, Soums and Bags. Rural people were given education on many new fields in order to improve their financial condition.

41. World Bank Report, 2004, p. 12.
42. UNDP(n.d), Mongolia, 2007, MDG progress.
43. Ibid.
44. Grant Assistance Report, by Asian Development Bank proposed Grant Assistance Mongolia: Early Childhood Education for Rural, Nomadic, and Migrant Children. Financed by the Japan Fund for Poverty Reduction Project Number: 42222, July 2009.
45. Ibid.
46. European Bank for Reconstruction and Development Strategy for Mongolia as approved by the Board of Directors meeting, 21 Octber 2009.
47. Post Yokohama Mid-Term Review of the East Asia and Pacific Regional commitment and Action Plan against Commercial Sexual Exploitation of Children (CSEC) Mongolian Country Progress Report November 2004.
48. Personal interview with Edward Thornton, Head, Christina Noble, 2009-2010.
49. Children and women in Mongolia current situation and future goals –eng. pdf UNICEF.
50. In 1990, Mongolia was opened to the outside world and basic human rights including freedom of religion were proclaimed in the new constitution. Not only Buddhism, but Christianity, Islam and Bahai religions were also given permits by City Council to practice their faith.

Measure for Rehabilitation 4

REHABILITATION BY NATIONAL COUNCIL FOR CHILD PROTECTION

Although government of Mongolia is facing economic difficulties yet it remains committed towards the children's issues. National Programme of Action for Children was endorsed by the Parliament[1] wherein child protection was specifically focused and addressed.

Fig. 4.1: Chairperson (right) of the National Council for Child Protection and her co-workers (Photo by Author)

According to the National Council for Child Protection, the problem of street children began in 1992 and NCCP officially started working on street children in the beginning of 2002. Data collection on the number of street children was done in the same year. Official figures state that from 1992 to 2002, there were approximately 2,000 children on the streets and by 2004 number decreased to 200. The decline trend owes to a number of reasons such as state run organizations who took initiatives to rehabilitate them. International NGO's and private care centres provided services to these children in care centres. Many of these children were resettled in the families. Moreover, the street children in the age group of 16 and above were registered, educated and given training in various skills in different centers. In recent years, their numbers have markedly reduced and only around fifty boys have been found hanging around on the streets. There are about forty of them who return home at nightfall. These are official figures and hardly tally with the unofficial figures provided by international organizations. Ulaanbaatar has two centres for these children; one is temporary night centre where children stay during the night, and another is a Day Care Shelter Centre installed by the government. International organizations are funding these centres.

In the beginning the impression was that unemployment of the parents and family members was the main reason behind children living on the streets, but now this problem is seen quite differently with multiple dimensions. Most of these children were abused and abandoned by their parents. As the problem was new, there were no professional social workers to look into the problem. After many years of struggle and with the help of International NGOs social work setup has been created that work and take care of them, primarily for their protection and survival and then training and rehabilitation.

The child protection programme is the flagship for 2007-2011.To promote the protective environment for children, the National Council of Child Protection is working on capacity building at *Soum*, *Bhag* and *Aimag* levels in coordination with NGOs since 2007. The focus is now seriously shifted to have a legal framework on child protection especially on violence, juvenile justice, trafficking of the children, sexual exploitation, abuse and neglect.

The lack of statistical data is hindering to ascertain the real number of these children and it is getting very hard to observe the movement of these children. To cope with problems, Council of Child Protection has four main programmes such as: (i) Data analyses and Information; (ii) Advocacy and Awareness; (iii) Legal and Regulatory system; and (iv) Capacity Building. The Council is trying to plan, monitor, institutionalize and implement the objectives. They are drafting future-related programmes to be completed by 2011. Once implemented by letter and spirit, it will be possible for the country to overcome this problem nationwide. However, there are many hurdles to achieve these goals. On the ground level the implementation process has been slow due to the lack of infrastructure, trained manpower and institutional coordination. However, NGOs are doing well in this regard.

The National Action Plan for the development and protection of children state that the condition of these children could be improved only by their active participation in the family chorus and communal activity. The key policy of, "Changing the World for Children with the Children", would work by allowing these children to join the organizations working for the children's issues. To address this dimension child protection centre has trained social workers, who have formulated projects with those children who were called street children and have grown to adulthood. These children were taken into confidence to actively participant in the discussions regarding the issues of street children. They are helping the social workers to categorize the street children. With the help of these children, National Child Protection Centre is collecting data on Street children and street working children. Social workers give different sort of services to these children like building trust, finding jobs for them establishing contacts and creating relationship with these children. Focus is on the issues like, tracing the families of these children, setup contacts, appraise the family situations and find the ways to reunite these children with the families. Street children are appended with a stigma of shame – this attitude is being changed through various awareness campaigns and different levels.

For last nine years NCCP is working on this issue and hopefully with the authority of National Council these goals can be accomplished. But the policies need be periodically renewed, for which Parliament and Council members are trying their best to remove the bureaucratic bottlenecks. *Ms. Togtokhnyam Mijiddorj,* the Chairperson, National Council of Child Protection said, "*We are like actors on the stage and it is the people who will tell us whether we performed or not; although it was hard but we think that after hard work around 2011 at least in Ulaanbaatar street children problem will disappear.*"[2]

MEASURES OF REHABILITATION BY NGOs

Save Children Fund[3]

This UK based organization's first priority in rehabilitation programme was to provide shelter to these children and take them off the streets. As far as child protection is concerned Save Children designed a two tier strategy assigned to two specialist teams: one for children's education and the other for child protection. The latter also looks after guaranteed rights of the children. Save the Children rehabilitation work started with providing emergency shelters for 125 street children at five self-managed campuses in Ulaanbaatar's poor suburbs in 1996 and is known as *khot ail* (the family unite) project.

Ten years ago Save Children established the child centre that focused on street children alone. Three centres provided services for children in *ger* areas in the outskirts of Ulaanbaatar city. These centres work from Monday to Friday to provide social services to the children. Focus is more on protection from child abuse.

Ms. Bolormaa an official of Save Children Fund revealed that although the number of street children is decreasing due to several reasons but there are new problems which are affecting the children. Problems associated with housing and infrastructural facilities creep up as soon as a new centre is established or an older one is being shifted to a new locality. She adds, "*We moved to this apartment area after housing in ger area in a double storied building. We had a quite big space there but it was quite a distance to the street children of the city. Visiting parents and families found it inconvenient. By some support from the British government we purchased an apartment, which is comparatively small. The apartment price is increasing every year and it is difficult to find such a big place. People in the cities did not like to have such centres in their neighbourhood. Vulnerable children living nearby are considered a sort of shame; we have to address that too. It took us 9 to 10 months to find this place. Apartment is small but we got connected to central heating and electricity.*"

Fig. 4.2: Author with the Save Children Fund (Photo by Author)

Infact Save Children receive six to twelve children on daily basis. Children are free to visit any time they like. Children are not forced to stay on; it is up to them because some children need to go out during the daytime to make money. Some of them are not very keen to stay all the time in the centre which provides meals once a day; children could take shower any time and utilize the laundry services too. Social workers assist them in such activities. The important component of the centres programme is to reunite the child with the family as majority of them have a family.

The social workers on an average work with ten children a month, establish contact with them and build confidence and trust. They work with the children in-groups or individually to reconnect broken relationship with their parents, and to listen to their experiences. Therefore, these social workers take six months to one year to build a healthy relationship, inculcate confidence to overcome the trauma children have gone through. Generally 19-20 children are accepted yearly for this programme in order to maintain the quality of connectivity and rehabilitation as it demands a lot of time and material support. Every year funds decrease because of global economic recession. In addition there is a difference of perceptions between the organizers and the donors. The latter have their priorities which they would not be prepared to compromise. The entire rehabilitation process is actually donor-driven.

Compared to other groups of the children the street children are quite different. Because of the trauma in their life and the rough times they had, it takes a lot of commitment, time and resources to develop rapport with them, to develop them and put them back into society and law abiding citizens. Therefore, it is important to build their personality and make them fit for participation in different spheres of the society. Involvement of these children in activities of social life is important. Their alienation is to be replaced by participation. Majority of these children are illiterate; physically and psychologically they are not adequately developed. Thus training is imparted to help them improve their body mobilization an atmosphere is created to establish friend circles and peer groups.

So far Save Children has been successful in re-uniting 20 children with their families. In some cases the children are away from their homes for a long time and they do not want to go back. Many of them do not have any family and express a desire to live an independent life.

"Whenever we want to re-unite the children we need to buy the Ger but now it costs one million tugricks and each year the price increases, land ownership and its transfer further complicates the situation. Previously there was collectivization and hence no need to own a patch of land, but after privatization, demand for land has increased manifold. We have to give them a Ger, find land and get them registered. It requires personal documents which most of the children do not possess. Frustrated by legal and administrative hiccups they prefer street life."[4] The socialist system was regulated from top to bottom; common people had no worry of their future but during transition people smart enough had access to the wealth and production avenues of the new system. They took advantage of free market but those who did not have any connections or any special skills and access to productive forces, were hard hit. Poverty, frustration, alcoholism and neglect in family maintenance are found to be significantly correlated; one variable

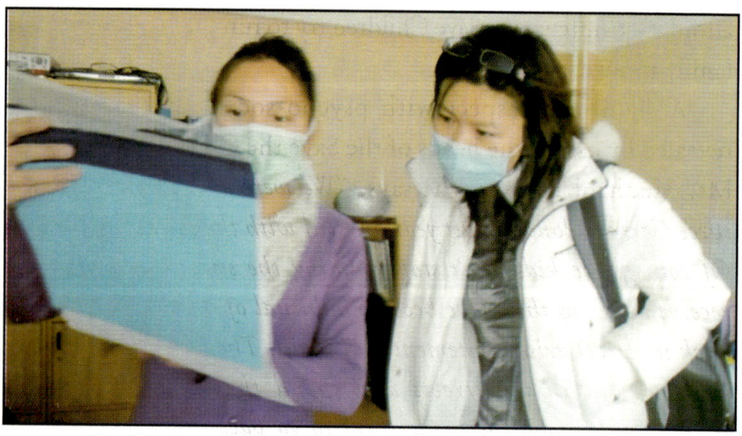

Fig. 4.3: Save Children Child Centre Head (Photo by Author)

leading to other and then their reinforcement and dynamics confusing.

In order to provide good service the centre re-defines and redrafts its policies every year. Save Children has also invested in the capacity building of local and non-government organizations and activists who are tackling the issues of street children at different levels. With the local government and NGOs it has intensified its work to trace children's families, establish contacts, assess family situations and explore ways to reunite families whenever and wherever feasible, introduce social work service and other support system for the children and their families.[5]

There are around 150 children, but annually Save Children gets 3,000 children which include repetitive counts i.e. when a child visits a centre for a number of times. If children stop coming to the centre all of a sudden, the centre tries to track them down. Children without a shelter are provided with a *Ger*. If the children have a family *Ger* they are motivated to stay at home with their parents. Most of them receive *Gers* from World Vision. This organization has large-scale programmes and centres in different regions of the countryside. A number of families who lose their *Gers* because they are unable to afford its maintenance, Save Children try to run these *Gers* by finding family to manage them.

A significant aspect with psycho-social implications was revealed by one of the heads of the Save the Children Fund centre Ms. Munhzul Hoovoi, she says, "*We were able to ascertain that three Gers we donated last year are still with the matching families. Of course, the kids don't stop roaming the streets even after they receive a Ger as they have become habitual of the practice. Getting back to streets arise excitement and thrill. They like the freedom of hanging out in the streets and spend the earned money. We try to intervene and persuade them to go back home. To a certain extent they enjoy this life with their friends or peer groups. Its alternative back home means living without electricity, food and heating. Although pressed into street life, they get infatuated to its offerings."*

Broken family system, maltreatment at the hands of stepfathers and stepmothers and physical abuse are revealed to be the main factors forcing children out to streets.

Centres organize a lot of group activities and give out prizes if children do well. Token prizes include certificates that are meant to motivate them to keep working hard. Centre is persistently working with the parents make them understand the multidimensional aspects of the problem and the role of family and parents.

Very few street children are ignorant of child centres. They gang up as soon as they find out that a member of a stronger, rival gang has entered their centre. They are well aware of the social structure of the centres and their power distribution. The Yalalt gang is the biggest and the most notorious. Some of them are now adults and have graduated to criminal status, prosecuted and imprisoned. After their release they again gang up and recruit newcomers. As most of them are selfish and do not take jokes and games in their real spirit. They earn money by washing cars for people, begging and collecting waste plastic bottles and litter. They are different from children who do honest labour and show positive signs of reform. Children who perform wide variety of productive tasks have the ultimate goal of going back to their families.

Some Brochures of Save Children Fund

To attract them to the centres and keep them off the streets Save Children distributes beautifully designed flyers with catchy slogans about their centre.

Fig. 4.4: Flyers with Catchy slogans

Naizaa, Chi Oolisichi bain uu?

найзаа, чи өлсөж байна уу?

My friend, are you hungry?

Darch eswel Gantsaardachi bain uu?

Даарч эсвэл ганцаардаж байна уу?

Are you cold or feeling lonely?

Hoolii Garaa Shalbalchii ,Yamar Neg Oubuchiin Tosuguii biz?

Хол гараа щалбааж ямар нэг овчин тусаагүй биз?

Have you injured your feet and hands or are you suffering with some incurable disease?

Haloon Osand Ormoor bain uu?

Халуун усанд ормоор байна уу?

Do you want to have a warm bath?

Чамайг сонсч ойлгож чадах минь, нэгэнтээ ярилцахыг хүсч байна уу?

Chamaig Sonsoch, Oligoch Chadag Hiin Negentei Yarultsakhiig Husechi bain uu?

Do you want to talk to somebody who could understand your feelings?

Fig. 4.5: From Save Children Fund

Above four cards are used for different purposes and are handed over to the children to get help from the centre. It reminds the children that it is a public place and must respect the rights of the other kids.

WORLD VISION[6]

Under the 'Gift a Ger' project in 2007, world vision has donated *Gers* to the families in 16 provinces who were in awful conditions. It has seven 'Light House centres' mostly in Ulaanbaatar, Darkhan and Selenge. Near the railway station in Ulaanbaatar, 250 children are living in Light House Centre. These houses host 4 or 5 children, from the streets, where house parents look after them. The state organizations, police and other institutions dealing with the issues of the children, bring them from the streets and World Vision gives them special projects. It works with the state agencies at national, *aimag* and *Soum* level. Programmes are organized in 18 provinces out of 21. These are like area development programme with which young people are trained in professional fields to generate their own income. Once these children get jobs they leave the houses.

To make these children independent they are involved in projects related to health and education. Lectures and seminars are organized on the human relationship, cohabitation and citizenship. Parents are imparted education on child protection, violence, abuse, social inequality and their responsibilities towards their children. Economic development programme provides building material to poor families to build their own houses. The handicraft project involves street children in imparting training in carpentry and sewing besides making tools for farming. In addition, children are provided loans and taught the technicalities of business. There are short term project on nutrition, healthcare, tuberculosis treatment, maternal health and first aid. These programmes are organized in collaboration with the local health organizations, therefore, contributing to health education.

Fig. 4.6: World Vision office Ulaanbaatar (Photo by Author)

Christian Noble[7]

Christian Noble has a *Ger* program under the name of '*Blue Sky Gers*'. These *Gers* are erected from the donations on a village pattern. In the *Ger* village there is a common house for all children. Attached to common *Ger* is a cooking house and dinning house, a theatre where Mongolian songs and music is taught on traditional Mongolian instruments. These *Gers* are like a family unit that serves the purpose of bringing self-confidence. Most of them are psychologically disturbed when initially brought in to *Ger* villages. Some are physically abused and *Blue Sky Gers* are trying to regain their lost trust, therefore, these *Gers* have become healing places for those who are in desperate need of love and care. A sense of belonging is inculcated in this desperate lot. Ten residential *Gers* put six children in each *Ger* with *Ger* mother and the mothers themselves are the single mothers who had a difficult past, such mothers are allowed to bring their own children too. They are the homeless women who get jobs and grow food on small plots and teach the children how to be self-sufficient.

This community, besides giving love and care, also gives a chance to these kids to settle down in their own secular culture. There is a school with a basketball court which is converted into skating court in winter. fortunately de-regularization and opening up of political system has led to clean sailing for builders. Government centres are quite tidy and clean. The overall situation is steadily showing improvement.

A sense of readjustment is instilled and these children are finding a new life for themselves, leaving behind their past shrouded with negative attitude, nightmare, antisocial tendencies and fatalistic attitudes.

Measures on Education by the Government

The Mongolian state, its officials and intelligentsia are convinced that reducing poverty through education is one of the time tested devise to eradicate various other social problems. Ardiin Erkh December 15th 2009 Ulaanbaatar, reports that "*In 1990 the number of educated street children were 87 per cent and after 9 years it reduced to 67 per cent.*" This report was based on a research depicting the alarming trend with regard to education.

With the help of NGOs, the government of Mongolia framed the policies to support the sustainable livelihood for its population. In order to reduce poverty the participation of civil society in different projects was encouraged. Emphasis was put on the role of education in fighting poverty and unemployment. Goals were set forth for the development of quality education. Access to education to both urban and rural population, with qualified teachers, better educational infrastructure and improvement in school buildings and dormitories particularly in rural areas is provided.[8]

Recently Japan Fund for Poverty Reduction (JFPR) in collaboration with Asian Development Bank focused on the education to children of poor herding families, migrant children and children from minorities.[9]

In post-Soviet period, there was like other social security privileges, free education had vanished and owing to harsh economic conditions, parents were not in a position to send their children to schools where fee had to be paid, books and stationery had to be purchased and all other expenses on schooling of children including their medical aid had to be provided by the parents themselves.

With no substantial industry support to Mongol economy, socio-economic situation worsened and survival was more important than the luxury of schooling. Mongol state and society was desperately trying to arrest the downslide.

National Centre of Children (NCC), Save the Children Fund, UNICENF, UNISCO are trying to address the problem and its manifestations. UNICEF spent 130,000 dollars for its three year project.[10] Many voluntary workers were recruited to help and contribute. The Minister of Education and Science *Mr. S. Tomorochir*, formulated a new law on education which gives more freedom to the individual than the state.[11] It shows a clear paradigm shift with regard to the status and role of state as an institution. With the *American Master Plan* and *Danida* project professionals were engaged to guide the Mongolian scholars and specialists to improve the quality of education and research work.

With the support of UNESCO, the Ministry of Education, Culture and Science (MECS) launched Education for All (EFA) in her national action plan in 2005. In 2006 and 2007 school feeding programme was launched for grade one to four. A comprehensive National Plan of Action for Children (NPAC) had been launched back in 1993 followed by a law on child protection in 1996-1997.

1999 education Act fixed school entrance age at 6 years and was implemented only in Ulaanbaatar. National Reproductive programme on student and adolescent health implementation period was set for 2002-2005. Ministry of Health and Social Welfare in collaboration with Ministry of Enlightenment piloted a Reproductive Health Education programme in 12 schools in Mongolia. 2010-2015 plan contain provision for National Health responsibility of the government for the health insurance of children less than18 years of age.[12]

EDUCATION AND SAVE CHILDREN FUND

Children's Education Team of Save Children Fund is helping government in eradication of illiteracy among children. Emphasis is laid on imparting quality education to specified target group of vulnerable children which include children with disabilities, children of nomadic families and children from minority groups from western part of Mongolia.

The projects like 'Working Children Project' offered many opportunities to these children through its small projects. Children are provided tools to ease their labour and to detach them from difficult hazardous jobs. They are encouraged to combine work and studies, enabling them to earn their living in safer and more productive ways. Efforts were made to disengage the children from illegal activities by expanding their educational and development opportunities, enrolling them in kindergartens, schools, informal educational institutes and vocational training institutions. Besides, training is provided to parents, teachers, local government officials, medical personnel and NGOs who arouse awareness and knowledge about social problems. Projects like summer camps, life skill training, fine art projects, video, social circus based on interests of children and ideas were implemented. The evaluation reveals positive effects on children's social and communication skills, innovative and creative thinking as well as self-confidence.

World Vision on Education

In the field of education both in rural and urban areas World Vision has built kindergartens and schools for the children who could not afford to go to school—stationeries, meals and clothing are provided to these children. The dropouts are given the chance to enrol in English language courses and computer schools, this has helped to decrease rate of dropouts. To create trust and a conducive social system, sponsored programmes have given children opportunities to live in an environment that gives them hope and facilitate their personality development.

Art work is considered as a tool of realignment to the society. Essay writing competitions are organized and every family is given a chance to participate. Topics are family related so as to assess how these children change and how they feel about their families. Work is mostly on community basis. World Vision has a big musical group called "Blue Sky" of street children who have become famous not only in Mongolia but have entertained the audiences in many parts of the world. They are very popular in China, Korea and many other countries.

Adiya Byambatseren, Co-Director, World Vision states that, "*We provide not only the care and belonging but address all other needs of such children. Now they have shelter, education and skills, we think that it is better for children to stay with their families than to stay in any other institute. International organizations provide the money, although global recession reduced funding of various projects but negotiations continue for refunding. World Vision Japan is contributing a lot. Foster parent programme in Mongolia, a new concept, is also improving and many organizations are working on it.*"

Christina Noble Children's Foundation and Education

The Christina Noble runs an education programme for the children who are detained in the prisons for petty crimes. The organization runs five principle programmes besides some auxiliary one. These programmes are clubbed as: i) boys prison programme and girls prison programme; ii) sponsorship and reintegrated classes; iii) Blue Skies Kindergarten; iv) bakery training; v) prison school programme. Most often children are imprisoned for poverty related crimes and most of them are illiterate. The education programme concentrates on basics reading, writing and arithmetic skills, they are also taught Mongolian language, art, and computer. The number of students who attended the classes in 2008 was 119. Students are encouraged to discuss their problems with teachers. While interacting with the inmates, this target group expressed a strong desire to get at least the higher secondary education that will enable them to get jobs. For girls too vocational training is given so as to make them economically empowered. Christina Noble runs healthcare programme education program and computer class in prison. The staff goes to prisons every day to teach the normal curriculum, a bakery installed in the prison is run by these kids.

The Christiana Noble also helps school dropouts to restart their education who could not afford it otherwise owing to financial difficulties. The sponsorship programme has 1,600 children on its rolls and the child who enters this program has to agree to attend the full time school and live in the home. This is done to keep them off the streets and in education.[13] The brothers and sisters of these children are also entitled to get free medical attention.

Most of the families of the target group are single. Single or divorced women who keep their children without a regular source of income fall under this category. They are quite desperate to receive the money after four weeks. Therefore, sponsor programme is a lifeline for these children. The study programme brings confidence to these children and keeps them going in desperate situations.

Christiana Noble has given education to many street kids during past twelve years ever since it started working in Mongolia. Sixty children of the centre attend normal state schools. In Elementary school no fee is charged besides school uniform, school bags and stationary is provided. Children are enrolled in the nearest school to their home. A new batch 7 of children is taken on yearly basis who after completion of the course move forward to state school. These children are supported with the school inspector programme. The inspector goes to these schools to make sure that children are continuing their education. Those students who continue to attend are given new uniform and school supplies. Every year 154 children are enrolled in the kindergarten out of which 60 street children are from the *Ger* district and all of them are given daily meals. Mr. Edward Thornton reveals that, "*for many of them it is the only decent meal they get. The donation is paid in kind and not in cash. The sponsors get all the details of the children, their progress and expenditure of the sponsored money.*"

Christina Noble has also summer holiday program where they keep these kids occupied with sports and community based activities.

MEASURES ON VIOLENCE

Against Children

The economic pressure on parents turns them to alcohol resulting in domestic violence and child abuse. Stressful family environs forces children out to the streets. Between 1999 and 2004, the number of newly registered children in the Child Address Identification centres went up 38 per cent. In 2004, there were 903 street children registered at the national level which is half the number registered in 2001 and majority of them had been subjected to abuse and violence of one or the other form. Child abuse has revealed a significant correlation with increased crime rate.

In the absence of a healthy community environment or protective family atmosphere, children used to go on their own ways and were linked with many criminal activities through gang culture on streets.

There is a separate law on domestic violence which was passed in 2004. Domestic violence is not exclusive to children; male and female family members are its victims. Meanwhile UNICEF worked with Save the Children Fund on the abolishment of corporal punishment in educational institutions.

State machinery and NGOs are working on many projects but funding is always a problem and concern. With the help of NGOs a national social security network was created to formulate policies and strategies with regard to specific issues. Infact NGOs only cannot fulfil the task, the State wants to coordinated efforts with NGOs in the form of joint ventures. Violence against Children Centre is coordinating with sub-centres at districts, sub-districts level. Now the efforts are more coordinated and organized and the chronic cases get referred to high ups of the hierarchy in concerned ministries.

Facts and figures of violence against street children are contradictory, inaccurate and unreliable. Thcsc arc complex issues, not easy to check and verified. The centre for violence against children established in October 2002 is the front line organizations specified to deal with the problem. Besides counselling abused children, the Centre has created children helpline service, which is used by other organization too. In addition a contact number is solely used for 24

Fig. 4.7: Pamphlet from Violence against Children Centre

hours by the organization. The biggest issue is violence against children in family and schools; bullying from peers as well as from teachers. Violence in classes and schools is difficult to track for the lack of reporting. NGOs are working on this and UNICEF also supports the government in its various measures to stop the violence in the school. Unfortunately there is lack of coordination among the ministries and organizations at various levels of policy formulation and its execution. UNICEF in many such working groups participates as an observer.

The Centre is consulted on several other issues too, they help the children through the peer counselling. During working days they teach the dropouts, but during summer holidays, summer resort campuses are used to work not only with the children but their families too.

Sometimes people come with their daughters who had been raped. Counselling is provided to such victims and their families on the issues of psycho-social and legal matters. One of the main objectives is to find out the causes of these problems through counselling sessions, discussions and lectures. It arranges classes to the parents on many issues including books on the forms of violence.

Forms of violence are grouped under four categories; one is abuse of neglect, second is rape, physical and mental abuse, third is forced prostitution, human trafficking and fourth is child labour. Corresponding to these categories four byelaws have been formulated. The officials are well versed with the norms and with laws. NGOs are supposed to study them and remain well aware of their interpretations. In addition statistical studies are done with regard to the number of children, who work for the families, excluding those who work as domestic help. Because of the paucity of the funds centre could survey only two districts of *Bayan olgi* and *Bayan zurik.* The survey revealed that 40 such children fall under one or the other categories of violence against children.

NGOs are informed and they move very fast. The Centre also looks into prostitution and other problems related to girl protection.

In future Centre for Violence Against Children hope to expand their services nationwide.

Measures for Juvenile Justice

A survey in 1991 showed that there were 733 minors involved in criminal cases which increased to 1,676 in 2001. The justice system in Mongolia is still based on Russian legal system that is harsh and primitive. According to the UNICEF reports of 2002 and 2004, the number of children involved in crime was higher than the cases registered or documented. Children are treated at par with adults. For example, according to the criminal law an adult has to remain in prison for maximum15 years and the same applies to minor. In the detention centres children suffer physical and emotional damage that feeds the cycle of crime.[14] The age of the children involved in crime is around 14 and 15 years and majority of the detainees languishing in prisons meant for adult criminals is 15 years old. The crime committed by these children is mainly theft and robbery under survival pressures. Legal proceedings show utter disregard to socio-economic compulsions and that the crimes might have been committed under survival pressures. A variation is evident between responses of male and female street children where boys particularly get influenced by criminal activities more than the girls. Many of the children who have grown up on the streets are instrumental in influencing the younger street children by transplanting criminal tendencies and tricks of the trade. A few children above the age of 16 are registered and put into the vocational schools and training centres. There is a concerted effort by the community on the *Hoorul* (assembly) level. Social workers, police, school teams, all work together for the child protection. Children are put on probationary period postponing the judicial trial for one year and during this period child is allowed to go to the school. However it is obligatory that these children have to go to police station every month and get registered. They are always at risk in the sense that if they get involved in any other crime, the law becomes very harsh for them. In the survey conducted by the

National Human Rights Centre (NHRC) in 2001 it was revealed that out of 70 children detained in the *Gants Hudag* detention centre, 60 per cent children had been detained without the legal assistance. Of the sentenced juvenile, 30 per cent tend to be illiterate and 10-15 per cent are orphans and children who run away from home.[15]

On policy level UNICEF is working on capacity building in collaboration with the Law School of National University and with Police Academy, Ulaanbaatar. It also imparts special training to keep track of follow ups, and to protect child rights. Focus is on service delivery to promote the models which really serve the children.

Although Mongolia has many NGOs for children working in the country but again their service is mostly limited to Ulaanbaatar. Juvenile justice committees have come under focuses which are community based. Since 2007 government representatives, police, judiciary officials as well as doctors, psychologists and teachers coordinate for comprehensive rehabilitation of target groups. UNICEF focuses on three western *Aimages: Hodv, Ouvs and Baingal* on district level. Some other *Aimages* are also picking up. Still it is not easy area to work but some positive results have been achieved.

Zorig Foundation

Zorig Foundation[16] is educating youth to take part in the democratic processes and contribute to the society in a healthy way. The foundation focuses on freedom and social Justice, transparency and accountability of state and the government.

The *Ariiden Erikh* Mongolian News paper of 15th December 2009, reported that in a meet on problems of the street children it was found that there are still 1,400 children living on the streets of Mongolia. There is no security from the government. Alcoholic parents are still the main reason for the children to leave their homes and despite good work done by the NGOs there is lack of coordination and communication among different agencies at different levels.

Fig. 4.8: Youth attending a lecture in the Office of Zorig Foundation

According to an official report there are more than 70,000 children doing hazardous and other petty jobs at the cost of their schooling, 700 children have been pushed to the crime. They are taken to the courts where harsh punishments are accorded for minor crimes. The 1,400 children have been abused physically and emotionally. According to Ch. Ayuruzana, City Police Official, Child Protection Cell, Ulaanbaatar there are 100 to 120 children who come to their cell and they hand over these children to the reformatory centres, amongst this lot there is a good number of street children. These centres as per law take care of these children, sometimes one kid comes to the cell for about 90 times. He adds that alcoholic parents are still the main reason for which the children leave the homes.

Sexual Exploitation and Trafficking of Children

> *"It is almost guaranteed that if girls go out onto the streets, they become victim to sexual abuse. The gang system sometimes provides a safety net for these girls. Nowadays these kids drink a lot—they are unable to handle their drunkenness. There are cases of 18-year-old girls being pregnant; Save Children centres help them with providing*

information and necessary documents. Save Children is educating these young mothers about the rights of their children besides taking up the issue with the administration and fellow NGOs. The state should be responsible for caring for these children until they are independent. Giving money to begging children is not the best way to deal with the problem as there is no guarantee that they use the money properly. It is better to give them food, donate to helping agencies, or direct the kids to rehabilitation centres. Our educational programs are not that effective because they only spend a small portion of their day with us."[17]

Child Labour, Save the Children Fund, World Vision, International Organization on Migration and Asian Foundation supported a study on trafficking, conducted by Mongolian state shows that the number of street children involved in trafficking is not alarming but it is very difficult to ascertain the actual figures. State and community organizations have started cooperating in order to prevent sexual exploitation of adolescent and minor girls. In 2002, Mongolia ratified the United Nations optional protocol to the convention on the rights of the child, the sale of children, child prostitution and child pornography. In 2003, national network of government and non-government organizations was established to raise public awareness on sexual exploitation of children and to strengthen the national capacity for analyzing and fighting child prostitution and trafficking.

In a survey, *sexually exploited girls emphasized their need for: a safer profession, availability of options for safe housing, returning home and obtaining psychological counselling and emotional support for recovery from the past exploitation experiences. However, child protection workers lack requisite knowledge and skills for helping girls who have been sexually abused and exploited. There is no official system of counselling and support in place for girls. NGO staff working in this field has raised awareness that there is no system for ameliorating the root cause which initially increased the risk for these girls to become victims of sexual exploitation. The factors leading to the syndrome are stress from poverty, living in poor households and an abusive family situation. There is dire need to provide assistance for the poor household, psychological support for distressed victim and her family and awareness about the impact of abuse in the home and in the community.*[18]

NOTES

1. National Programme of Action.
2. Personal interview.
3. Save Children Fund is an International NGO.Since past 15 years it is working in Mongolia. However, Save UK decided to close its programme at the end of July 2009 and its endeavours were taken over by Save Children Japan.
4. Personal interview with Ms. BolormaaGulgou Child Protection Programme Officer Save Children Fund.
5. Save Children were able to reunite some 180 children with their families during the period 2003 to 2008, personal interview.
6. World Vision office was inaugurated in 1993 in Gobi Altai Aimag but it officially started working with the kindergarten program 1995. In 1997 street children programme was included as a special agenda. At the movement it is working with the 1000 children and their families.
7. Christina Noble Children Foundation was established by Christina who is an Irish Lady. She too had a difficult past, was raped when she was very young. She set her goal to work for the venerable children in Vietnam and Mongolia. The foundation has done a commendable job in specialized rehabilitation drives across the globe.
8. International Monetary Fund November 2005, IMF country report 05/405 http://www.imf.org
9. ADB(Asian Development Bank), Grant Assistance Report, proposed Grant Assistance Mongolia: Early Childhood Education for Rural, Nomadic, and Migrant children (Financed by the Japan Fund for Poverty Reduction) project number 42222 July 2009.
10. Mongolian Messenger, 1999.
11. Ibid.
12. Finding of the Worst Form of Child Labour-Mongolia 10th Sept 2009, www/unhcr/org/refworld/docid/9accesed 7march 2010) 4aba3edoc-html
13. "Sponsor sends 29 dollars per month. From this amount, management keeps four. Out of four dollars two dollars each are spent on staff that operates child sponsorship programmes and two go to the medical programme. In this medical programme sponsored children get medical aid. Remaining 25 dollars are given

to the children in cash every month," says Mr. Edward Thornton of the Foundation.

14. http://www.uncief.org/infobycountry/mongolia_41147.html
15. Situation Analysis of the Children and Women in Mongolia, NHRC, 2003, p. 73.
16. Zorig Foundation was founded after the name of Late Mr Sanjaasureniin Zorig who was murdered in 1998.
    He was a Parliament member and Minister of Infrastructure Development, Mongolia. It is said that he was instrumental in bringing the democratic change in the country. Born in an elite Buryat family. Received his higher education in Moscow. During my student days in Ulaanbaatar National University, I have spent most of my weekends in this family in 1981.
17. Ms. Munhzul Hoovoi of Save the Children Fund in an exclusive interview with the investigator.
18. Situation Analysis of Children and Women in Mongolia, UNICEF Mongolia, Ulaanbaatar, 2007, pp. 66-67.

Recommendations 5

A major social problem of street children has overtaken Mongol society after fall of communism in 1991. Norms of healthy and vibrant social order do not permit aberration of the kind we have stated in this book. Mongolian government and civil society at large are bound to reform society and root out the aberration. Although there are rich people in Mongolia but Mongols do not like to give money as giving means giving away the luck. They don't give money to the beggar, as it will bring bad luck it has the cultural thing as in Lamaism they say if you wash, you wash your happiness.[1] It will as such be the duty of the state machinery to eradicate the social problem. The state machinery is conscious of the urgent need to rehabilitate and reintegrate the street children and arrest new social pathology lest the situation develop into major crisis. Some concrete steps have been taken in this regard. For example The Children's Address Identification Center goes into the streets once a week and collects children who are lost. If they are over sixteen, they don't take them. They also take them to their homes if they provide an address. Because they don't have any professional social workers, they just take the kids to their homes without solving any of the problems that have caused the children to go out into the streets. As a consequence, their problems are not solved and they go back into the streets. Therefore, center has to do more careful analyses of the families and to work with them. Similarly NGOs mandated to work for the helpless children are also involved in their rehabilitation. What therefore is the need is education, healthcare, employment and psycho-social belonging mechanisms are to be placed in a manner that caters the basic requirements. Many Mongolian and international agencies are looking into these problems and their manifestations. On the basis of observation the investigator has come up with some humble recommendations. However, it is to be mentioned that the generalizations and recommendations pertain specifically to the study area. What could be recommended for speedy and viable solution to the case of Mongol street children may be summed up as follows:

a) It is very important that once the street children come of age, they are provided with employment and their lives are monitored for next ten years to prevent relapses and that they do not fall victim to the inferiority complex or discrimination.

b) Street children put in camps should not be left to isolation or segregation, instead a healthy exposure of their talent need to be integrated into the main body of Mongol society. They should be involved in cultural and social activities that give them the feel of belonging and being part of Mongolian society.

c) The state should undertake formal and legal matrimony of street children once they come of age, whether in coordination committee comprising of representatives of the government agencies, NGOs and civil society should be formed to educate Mongol men and women on observing strict moral code that sanctifies legalized matrimony as the only institution of producing offspring. This will hold both parents responsible for their children. The trespass to this norm shall be made liable to penal action.

d) Premarital and extramarital sex leads to insecure future for woman and the resultant child. An awareness campaign is to be lodged against such practices.

e) Local authorities in respective Soums shall generate and pool up their own resources in addition to NGOs funding. Organizations should coordinate their efforts to reunite these children to their families, give counseling and educate them about parental responsibilities.

f) Government of Mongolia and administration has to coordinate with International NGOs more often to formulate poverty reduction schemes which ultimately lead to healthy family atmosphere and put a halt to the continuous supply of children to the streets.

g) Herder families need to be made aware of their responsibilities towards the education of their children. As Mongolia is a young nation, the social welfare system has to be improved to achieve their goals in education. A viable cheap and indigenous welfare system has to replace the bygone Russian system. Besides, community initiatives at all levels are to be encouraged.

h) Infrastructure has to be taken care too. Psychological support for distressed families and children is call of the hour. Therefore, civil society, intellectual elite, poets, writers, print and electronic media has to take lead so that the benefits of various government and non-government measures reach the target groups in time of need.

i) As Mongolia is a country of young population, education sector has to be taken care off. The positive thing is that Mongolian people in the age group of 40-50 is literate, therefore, it is highly possible for the Mongolian government to bring back its youth to education and national reconstruction. Fortunately this very group is running administrative machinery and policy planning at the highest level. The encouraging part is that women and children are prepared to join schools. Policies and coordination in this sector is also important. School buildings have to be renovated and qualified teachers have to be trained. Their salaries need to be enhanced both in urban as well as in rural areas.

j) As the Mongolian population is scattered and sparsely settled over a vast area, it makes organization and regularization of educational activities very difficult. Therefore, an alternative is to be sought by bringing specialists in education together to redraft curriculum and redesign educational activities for academic year.

k) After an experimentation market economy and democracy for two decades the Mongolian government has to solve its problems rather than to be dependent on foreign aid, which follows alongwith many compromises on sovereignty and freedom of action. The foreign investments and grant-in-aid especially from US, Europe and Japan is to be subjected to transparency and accountability measures.[2]

l) As European experts have replaced Soviets, it is suggested that the Mongolian government train its own people on priority basis to generate native crop of human resource, who are more accustomed to culture and sensitive to the Mongol problems.

m) There is a need to establish more alternative care centres, besides educating general public to promote foster parenthood.

n) A coordinated and multiple tier documentation is needed to generate accurate and reliable data vis-à-vis number of orphans, alcoholics, divorces, single mothers etc. which will facilitate the state government and concerned organizations to form policy of rehabilitation and strategies to reach their goals.

o) Coordination should be improved among the working groups in ministry of Justice and the proposed amendments need to be finalized which are still in reviewing process.

p) A campaign should be launched in Mongolia, prompting rich and prosperous families to adopt a kid from the street children and bring him up as their own. The Mongolian society should take it as a national responsibility. Modalities for a such practice can be charted out in consultation with various agencies involved in the rehabilitation endeavour.

NOTES

1. *Society of Mongolia with special reference to religion and culture* by Maqsooda Sarfi 1996 Center of Central Asian Studies Kashmir University Sairbeen offset press Burzulla,Sanantnagar, p. 92.
2. Japan obviously for its own political gains show all the love to bestow upon not only to Mongolia but whole Central Asian newly formed states.

Bibliography

Balhaajav, Ts, *Contribution of the Mongols to World Civilization*, Ulaanbaatar, 1995.

Batbayar, Ts, *Modern Mongolia: A Concise History*, Ulaanbaatar,1996.

Batbayar, Ts, *Openness and Economic Security: Some Policy Issues, Mongolias External Relations and Regional Economic Cooperation*, National Institute of Research Advancement, Tokyo, 1996.

Bewden, C. R., *The Modern History of Mongolia*, Weidenfeld and Nicholson, London, 1968.

Bira, Sh., Mongol Empire and the East West Relations, Mongolia (*Culture, Economy and Politics*) Khama Publishers, New Delhi, 1992.

Buruun, O. and O. Odgaard, A Society and Economy in Transition, *Mongolia in Transition*, Curzon Press 1996.

Bruun, O., The Herding Household: Economy and Organization, *Mongolia in Transition*, Curzon press, 1996.

Bugd Nairamdakh Mongol Ard Ulsiin Tuukh (History of the Mongolian Peoples Republic); Ulaanbaatar, 1966.

Chikyuu no Arukikata, Mongoru (97-98), Vol. 42, Diamond-Big Co., Ltd., Tokyo, 1997 (5th edition).

Dashdondov, H., "Progressive Changes in the Socio-economic Development of the MPR (1921-1988)," *India and Mongolia: Experience and Interaction*, Scholars Publishing Forum, New Delhi, 1991.

Dashpurev, D, Democratization of Mongolian Society, *Mongolia (Culture, Economy and Politics)*, Khama Publishers, New Delhi 1992.

Enkhee, "Development of foreign Trade in Mongolia in Recent Years and the Role of Trade and Economic Relations Between China and Mongolia in Regional Cooperation", *Mongolia's External Economic Relations and Regional Economic Cooperation*, 1996.

Gilberg, R. and J.O. Svantesson, "The Mongols, Their Land and History," *Mongolia in Tranisition*, Curzon Press, 1996 pp. 5-22.

Goldstein, M.C. and C. M. Beall, *The Changing World of Mongolia's Nomads*, University of California press, Berkeley and Los Angeles, 1994.

Griffin, Keith., "Economic Strategy during the Transition," *Poverty and the Transition to a Market Economy in Mongolia*, St. Martin's Press, 1995.

Jaadamba, S., and S. H. Sharavaaldi, *Agricultural Cooperatives in the Mongolian Peoples Republic*, Ministry of Agriculture, Ulaanbaatar, 1966.

Lhagva, S., "International Trade Reform of Mongolia," *Mongolia's External Economic Relations and Regional Economic Cooperation*, 1996.

Maqsooda, S., *Impact of Socialism on the Contemporary Society of Mongolia with Special Reference to Religion and Culturea :*, Center of Central Asian Studies, University of Kashmir, 1995.

Mongolian Economy and Society in 1996, State Statistical Office of Mongolia, Ulaanbaatar, 1997.

Mongolian National Programme of Action for Development of Children in 1990's, Government of Mongolia, 1993.

Natsagdorj, Sh., *Manj Erkhshild Baisan Uyiin Khakkhiin Kharankhui Tuukh* (The Dark History of Khalkhas during the Rule of Manchus), Ulaabaatar, 1963.

Natsagdorj, Sh., *Bugd Nairamdakh Mongol Ard Ulsiin Soyoliin Tuukh* (The Cultural History of Mongolian Peoples Republic), Ulaanbaatar, 1981.

Sanjdorj, M., *Manchu Chinese Colonial Rule in Northern Mongolia* (translated from the Mongolian and annotated by Urgunge Onon, prefaced by Owen Latttimore), 1963.

School Drop Out in Mongolia, United Nations International Children's Fund.

Sheehy, D. P., "Sustainable Livestock Use of Pastoral Resources," *Mongolia in Transition*, Curzon Press, 1996.

Shirendev, P., *Mongol Ardiin Khubisgaliin Tuukh* (History of the Mongolian Peoples Revolution), Ulaanbaatar, 1969.

Skapa, B., and A. F., Benwell, "Women and Poverty During the Transition," *Mongolia in Transition.*, Curzon Press, 1996.

Smith, Sh., "Human Capital Formation Under Conditions of Actue Resource Scarcity," *Poverty and the Transition to a Market Economy in Mongolia*, St. Martins Press, 1995.

Swift, J., "Rural Development: The Live Stock Sector," *Poverty and the Transition to a Market Economy in Mongolia*, St. Martin's Press, 1995.

Thayar, N. "Mongolia Forward Steppe," *Far Eastern Economic Review*, March 27, 1997.

The Trade Unions of Mongolia Today, Ulaanbaatar, 1981.

Tesrel, B., *Dorvon Oirad ba Oriadiin kholboond Bagtakh Undesten Yastnuudiin Ugsaa Tuukhiin Zarim Asuudal*, Ulaanbaatar, 1997.

Uradyan E. Bulag., *Nationalism and Hybridity in Mongolia*, Clarendon Press, Oxford, 1998.

References

Asian Outreach, 2008 *Mongolia,* http://www.asianoutreach.org.nz/asian%2Boutreach/page.php%3Fpage%3D21

Becky Hsu, Amy Reynolds, Conrad Hackett, James Gibbon, "Estimating the Religious Composition for All Nations: An Empirical Assessment of the World Christian Database," *Journal for the Scientific Study of Religion*, 2008.

B. Mabaera, N. Naranbat, P. Dhliwayo, H. L. Rieder, "Efficiency of Serial Smear Examinations in excluding Sputum Smear-positive Tuberculosis," *The International Journal of Tuberculosis and Lung Disease,* 2006.

Central Intelligence Agency, 2009, *Mongolia, Chiefs of States and Cabinet Members,* https://www.cia.gov/library/publications/world-leaders-1/world-leaders-m/mongolia.html

Ebright J.R., Altantsetseg T., Oyungerel R. (2003) *Emerging infectious diseases in Mongolia.* Emerg Infect Dis.

Gerard A. Postiglione and Jason Tan., *Going to School in East Asia,* New York, 2007.

Kachondham Y., Dhanamitta S., Oyunbileg M., Brown L., *Child Health and Nutritional Status in Ulaanbaatar, Mongolia: A Preliminary Assessment,* Asia Pacific J Public Health 1992/1993.

Kishigbuyan D. and Bundii R., *School Dropouts in Mongolia: Mid-Decade Review of Progress Towards Education,* United Nations Educational, Scientific, and Cultural Organization, 1996, *http://www.eric.ed.gov:80/ERICDocs/data/ericdocs2sql/content_storage_01/0000019b/80/17/25/cc.pdf*

Maitreya Charity Mongolia, 2008 *http://www.maitreyacharity.org*

Manaseki S., *Mongolia: A Health System in Transition.* BMJ, 1993.

Ministry of Health, *Health Indicators,* 2005.

Ministry of Health, *Mongolia Health Informatin System: Assessment Report,* 2008, *http://www.who.int/healthmetrics/library/countries/hmn_mng_hisassessment.pdf*

Riding World, *Mongolia,* 2009, www.ridingworld.com/ mongolia/

Statistical Yearbook for Asia and the Pacific, *Educational Outcomes,* 2008, *http://www.unescap.org/STAT/ data/syb2008/13-Educational-outcomes.pdf*

Selection on Asian Statistics, *Mongolia, http://www.paulnoll.com/China/Asia-Stats/index.html*

UNDP. (n.d.). *Mongolia.* (2007). MDG Monitor.

UNDP (n.d). *Mongolia.* (2007). MDG Progress.

UNDP (n.d). *Mongolia* (2007), National Report.

UNDP. (2008). *Mongolia.* 2007/2008 Human Development Report.

UNICEF. (n.d.), *Every Child has the Right to Healthy Growth: Health and Nutrition,* 2002, *http://www.unicef.org/mongolia/UNICEF_factsheet_eng.pdf*

UNICEF. (n.d.), *Mongolia: Learning Years, http://www.unicef.org/mongolia/children_2579.html*

World Bank. (n.d.), *Public Financing of Education in Mongolia: Equity and Efficiency Implications,* 2006, *http://siteresources.worldbank.org/MONGOLIAEXTN/Resources/Public_Education_Financing_Mongolia_2006.pdf*

World Health Organization, *World Health Statistics,* 2006, *WHO Statistical Information System: http://apps.who.int/whosis/data/Search.jsp*

Glossary

Aimag – The largest administrative division
Aduu – Horse
Azraga – Breeding Horse
Arats – Peasants (Cattle breeders in Mongolia)
Ariin Khaalag – Rear Door
Albat Arat – Common lay men
Ajilchin – Workers
Bator – Hero
Bilge – Wise
Bagush – Teacher
Bag – Ruler Sub-district
Daaga – Two year old horse
Dund Khun – Middle class people
Darga – Owner
Ezen – Lord
Ger – Traditional Mongolian round tent
Guu – Mare
Golomt – Hearth
Hoorul – Assembly
Khyazaalang – Four year old horse
Khar Khun – Lower class
Khamdjilga Aral – Bondage (serfs)
Khot ail – Group of families

Khokh – Blue colour

Mori – Horse

Neg nutgiin khun – People from the same place

Negdels – Cooperatives, Associations, Unions

Neg usniitan – Communities of one water

Noyons – Nobles

Shavinars – Personal serfs

Sums – Districts

Shudleng – Three year old horse

Soyoolong – Five year old horse

Sain Khun – High class

Tajis – Noblemen

Tavan Khoshuu mal – Five kinds of animals

Tsagaan – White color

Torson nutag – Birth place

Togrock – Mongolian Currency

Unaga – One year old horse

Ulus – State

Zuud – Snow storm

Index